EVERYTHING ABLAZE

Everything Ablaze

MEDITATING ON THE MYSTICAL VISION OF TEILHARD DE CHARDIN

DAVID RICHO

Paulist Press
New York / Mahwah, NJ

Cover image by Drakonova/Shutterstock.com
Cover and book design by Lynn Else

Library of Congress Cataloging-in-Publication Data
Names: Richo, David, 1940– author.
Title: Everything ablaze : meditating on the mystical vision of Teilhard de Chardin / David Richo.
Description: New York : Paulist Press, 2017. | Includes bibliographical references.
Identifiers: LCCN 2017001347 (print) | LCCN 2017015716 (ebook) | ISBN 9781587687020 (ebook) | ISBN 9780809153367 (pbk. : alk. paper)
Subjects: LCSH: Teilhard de Chardin, Pierre. | Mysticism—History—20th century. | Catholic Church—Doctrines—History—20th century.
Classification: LCC BX4705.T39 (ebook) | LCC BX4705.T39 R53 2017 (print) | DDC 248.2/2092—dc23
LC record available at https://lccn.loc.gov/2017001347

ISBN 978-0-8091-5336-7 (paperback)
ISBN 978-1-58768-702-0 (e-book)

Published by Paulist Press
997 Macarthur Boulevard
Mahwah, New Jersey 07430

www.paulistpress.com

Printed and bound in the
United States of America

For my fellow Associates of the Sacred Heart
and for
Teilhard and Pope Francis

———————

Truth has to appear only once,
in one single mind,
for it to be impossible for anything ever
to prevent it from spreading universally and setting
everything ablaze.
—Pierre Teilhard de Chardin, *The Heart of Matter*

CONTENTS

CONTENTS

PREFACE

*What is it that breathes fire into the equations and makes
a universe for them to describe?*

—Stephen Hawking, *A Brief History of Time*

*I have set the world on fire, and behold, I am watching
over it until it comes to a full blaze.*

—Gospel of Thomas

Pierre Teilhard de Chardin, a descendant of Voltaire and,
according to family lore, distantly of Pascal, was born in
France in 1881. He was a Jesuit priest, theologian, and geologist-
paleontologist. He taught at universities in Paris and Cairo.
Teilhard's work was judged as not in keeping with the magisterial
teachings of the Church. This meant he was not permitted to teach
theology for much of his professional life. Instead, he worked as
a scientist in China for many years. His writings from 1924 and
1955 were published posthumously. Teilhard died in New York
City on Easter Sunday, 1955.

We begin with a brief exploration of Teilhard's work, mysticism, and contemplation as the mystic's style of prayer. We then
focus on specific themes in Teilhard's books, letters, and essays
that highlight his love for the cosmos and his nature-suffused
mysticism. In each chapter, we begin with an explanatory yet also

meditative introduction to the topic. We then examine intently one quotation from Teilhard along with my own meditative response. This is followed by a prayer that asks for the grace to practice what has emerged in the meditation.

Next are several more quotations from Teilhard, chosen because they have mystical themes that expand on the topic at hand. You are invited to choose one or more quotations that inspire you, and then write your own meditative responses and personal prayers in your journal.

To my great joy and surprise, the quotations were richly evocative in personal ways, opening me to new realizations; visions and intuitions developed from contemplating Teilhard's words but were not tied entirely to them. Using this free-flowing style of response may allow a quotation to lead you, too, in unique directions. This is how meditation can be more than pondering; it can move you forward on your personal journey.

At the completion of the book, it is my hope that you will have a deeper sense of Teilhard's mysticism and of your own. You will have begun or expanded an evolutionary mystical spirituality, a sumptuous result of meditating on and with Teilhard.

Contemporary interest in Teilhard's work manifests the evolutionary mysticism he taught and forecasted. We can learn to apply his ideas and visions to our daily life. This is conscious evolution, a presence in the world as members of Christ's Body. Indeed, we are alive today to cocreate—through him, with him, in him, and as him—the future he came to proclaim. Now we are evolution become *intentional*.

Evolution for Teilhard is a continuous move toward the fullness of the risen Christ, the cosmic human, the divine human, a universal consciousness drawing all to universal convergence and connectedness. Teilhard shows us a path to such a glorious transformation. His mysticism, which was firmly grounded in contemporary scientific research, presents a vision of the cosmos as full of divine life. This is Christ, incarnate in matter, calling us to union with him through matter. A meditative focus on Teilhard's words opens us to the mysterious forces in the universe that continually reveal God's face. Our calling is to join in the momentum of our evolving universe so we can present that face to the world. We do this in all we are and find it everywhere we are. We also delightedly find out who we are because a calling always reveals our potential.

A mystic is continually discovering new realizations about who and what God is, and finding new ways of making contact with God. Each quotation and meditation in this book does the same; we are meeting God in new ways, with new names and with new depths of intimacy.

Sometimes we are taken with Teilhard's statements without fully understanding them. That doesn't matter. Our appreciation shows that an opening has occurred within us. Teilhard's words serve as kindling for an evolutionary spirituality to be ignited in us. Our best response is a yes to the grace of finally seeing and always finding everything ablaze.

In selecting this book, something has already awakened in you. It goes back to an ancient longing, though you might never have known how to put it into words. It is a longing for the goal and prize of a spirituality that transcends personal enlightenment or individual transformation. It is a longing to participate in a planetary Pentecost of universal love. It is a grace in us to desire a love this big, and graces are everywhere waiting for it to happen in us.

On a personal note, writing this book, more than any other, has had a powerful effect on my own faith. Pondering Teilhard— and Pope Francis, who is often quoted in this book—has given me a richer sense of how I, others, and the planet are connected to Christ's redemptive work. Consequently, I have found a deeper sense of who Christ is, what my faith in him is really about, and what it asks of me. I can now appreciate more *how* "God so loved the world." For these luminous graces, I thank the Holy Spirit, and I sincerely hope that this book enriches and expands you fellow pilgrims, so that your faith becomes richly cosmic in its scope and limitlessly loving in its reach.

> For all our limitations, gestures of generosity, solidarity and care cannot but well up within us, since we were made for love.
>
> —Pope Francis, *Laudato Si'*

ABBREVIATIONS

BE   *Building the Earth*, Dimension Books, 1965.

CE   *Christianity and Evolution*, Harcourt Brace, Jovanovich, Inc., 1969.

FM   *The Future of Man*, Harper and Row, 1964.

DM   *The Divine Milieu*, Harper and Row, 1960.

HM   *The Heart of Matter*, Harcourt Brace and Co., 1978.

HU   *Hymn of the Universe*, Harper and Row, 1961.

LT   *Letters from a Traveller*, Collins, 1962.

OS   *On Suffering*, Harper and Row, 1974.

PM   *The Phenomenon of Man*, Harper and Row, 1959; also known as *The Human Phenomenon*, Sussex Academy Press, 2003.

SC   *Science and Christ*, Harper and Row, 1968.

TF   *Toward the Future*, Harcourt Brace Jovanovich, 1974.

WTW   *Writings in Time of War*, Harper and Row, 1968.

INTRODUCTION

Teilhard as Scientist and Mystic

*All evolution is the progressive self-revelation of the
One to itself.*

—Sri Aurobindo, *Man in Evolution*

In his appreciation of evolution, Teilhard was influenced by the French philosopher Henri Bergson, whose vision of evolution went beyond that of Darwin. He spoke of a driving force, an *élan vital*, a direction, a meaning in evolution beyond the survival of species. To Bergson, evolution is not just a sequence of natural events that makes the world what it is. Evolution for Bergson was an ongoing and exciting story. This led Teilhard to a spiritually rich realization: the *élan vital* of evolution is Christic. The risen Christ is the direction and meaning of evolution. In this perspective, evolution is not only about how things change to adapt to new environments, but how they grow in the likeness of Christ, the origin and goal of the process. Evolution is not only about more connection, as in the herding instinct, but about more caring connection, as in the love instinct.

1

Teilhard saw the cosmos in Christ, made in his image, made so he could bring a new form of light into time and space. We notice this same mystical realization in the Gospel of John: "He was in the beginning with God. All things came into being through him….The true light, which enlightens everyone, was coming into the world" (1:2–3, 9). The proclamation, "Let there be light" on the first page of Genesis was a forecast of what is completed on the first page of John's Gospel. Christ confirms this when he says, "I am the light of the world" (John 8:12).

From a spiritually evolutionary perspective, Genesis is a beginning and a becoming too. Creation is still in progress toward becoming the fully extended Body of Christ, "the measure of the full stature of Christ….But speaking the truth in love, we must grow up in every way into him who is the head, into Christ, from whom the whole body, joined and knit together by every ligament with which it is equipped, as each part is working properly, promotes the body's growth in building itself up in love" (Eph 4:13, 15–16).

The universe is in progress/birth, which Teilhard calls "cosmogenesis," the ordering of the evolving world. He also shows us the interior essence of evolution: God spiritualizing matter, which he calls "Christogenesis," the progress/birth of Christ. This is the equivalent of love spiritualizing matter.

Christogenesis means "Christ alive in all things as cause, purpose, and fulfillment." Both cosmogenesis and Christogenesis are one. What nature is up to is what Christ is up to. Nature does what it does in the ever-expanding Christ; the incarnate Christ does what he does in an ever-evolving natural world.

The universe has, as its purpose, to reach what Teilhard calls the "Omega," the triumph of *agape*, the culmination of human history. *Agape* is selfless and universal love. Creation happened so that *God is love* could be the only three words left to say. Thus, Omega is a threshold to a "theosphere," the divine in matter— love as the convergence of all that is. It is also the force that pulls

2

forward the evolutionary processes on a daily basis. In Teilhard's view, we evolve because of the force of attraction of Omega, ultimate love, tugging at our lives. Without Omega, there is no evolutionary movement.

Teilhard encountered the presence of God, the divine Love that animates all things, in matter. Our calling, in his view, is not to turn from the world to God but to turn to God in the world. This is how we find the fulfillment of our lifetime longing for love without reserve. Teilhard proposed that evolution moves toward this divine goal by having more and more *complexity*, more and more *consciousness*, and more and more *convergence*. We might say that these three elements of evolution are a way of saying, "Holy, holy, holy!"

Teilhard used the word "noosphere" based on *nous*, a Greek word for knowledge. He imagined the earth to have a thinking layer around it, an invisible envelope of consciousness. This global mind contains the sum total of humanity's interior life, providing the ground for the next advance in the pageant of evolution. Likewise, mind is a quality of matter, so for Teilhard, there is consciousness not only in us but in all things. This was not a new realization. The ancient Greek philosopher Pythagoras taught that the universe has an intelligence.

Teilhard imagined the noosphere to be emerging from the biosphere, the vast web of physical life across our planet. The noosphere expands with each century in personal and planetary consciousness. It is not simply a collection of individual thoughts. It is interactive and holographic, happening now among all of us, larger than any of us, including all of us. Teilhard would certainly have recognized the internet as an expression of universal interconnectivity.

The cycle of evolution begins with divergence, things becoming differentiated. Then it moves to convergence, unification, wholeness. This completion or wholeness resembles what St. Paul referred to as the "Pleroma," the fulfillment of all things in Christ. In the Omega moment, the Pleroma happens simultaneously with the Parousia, a universal participation in God's life at the second coming of Christ. The Pleroma is the completion of Christ's salvific work. The Parousia is the coming of his new world of justice, peace, and love. To pray, "Thy kingdom come!" is to welcome both the Pleroma and Parousia, that is, to welcome the Omega point of evolution. It is *point* as in "pointer and purpose."

Omega is both the fulfillment of all that is and the inclusion of all of us in divine life, a restoration of all things in Christ, "who must remain in heaven until the time of universal restoration that God announced long ago through his holy prophets" (Acts 3:21). All of this is ultimately a mystery, so there are no words that can describe "what no eye has seen, nor ear heard, nor the human heart conceived" (1 Cor 2:9).

For Teilhard, evolution comes to a conclusion, Omega, though he also says, "I cannot admit that life meets a final check" (SC). Indeed, in our recent appreciation of cosmology, we foresee no final version of the cosmos. Richard Rohr writes, "The Easter Mystery says that the true apocalyptic message is not 'The end is near!' but 'The beginning is always happening!' Power cannot see that. Love can see nothing else."[1] We do not have to see Omega as an ending. We might prefer to appreciate every moment as an Alpha-Omega, a beginning and a completion. We are then always beginning and always already arrived. We recall St. Augustine in his *Confessions* referring to God as "ever ancient, ever new." What brought all to life as new in the Big Bang, the bounding ahead, is now past yet continuing to happen and ever arcing into the future.

Spirit and matter are singing in harmony. They are two notes of a single divine chord. They reflect two central themes of Christian faith, the incarnation and Pentecost. In both, two become one. In the incarnation, divine and human, spirit and matter, come together. At Pentecost, the risen Christ becomes Church, the community of faith. Our spirituality is incarnational *and* pentecostal because of an unending unity of spirit and matter, of individual and community, in one mystical harmony. Cosmic faith is attuning to this harmony of all that is and all we are at a soul level. Shakespeare saw this connection in *The Merchant of Venice*:

> Soft stillness and the night
> Become the touches of sweet harmony....
> Such harmony is in immortal souls.

> (Act 5, Scene 1, 54–55, 61)

In a moment of harmonious attunement, that is, when we feel the cosmic, divine, and human combined as one energy within ourselves, we experience full communion with all that is God.

The phrase "one energy" reminds us of Teilhard's words in *The Human Phenomenon*: "Somehow or other, there must be a single energy operating in the world." Oneness is a scientific realization, not only a mystical one. For instance, we are one in the sense that we all share the same laws of physics. There is no dichotomy between us and the universe or between us and anything. Likewise, using scientific terms, we might say that at death our soul does not escape from our body in a dualistic way. As things are composed of waves and particles, our body/matter is transformed at death. We become more wave than particle. Mystically, God is the ocean of waves of all worlds.

Physics uses the term *entanglement* to show a bond that endures in separation and has no finality. It is nonlocal, operating irrespectively of the physical distance between things. This also reflects the theological mystery of the Communion of Saints as an unending connection between those who are alive and those who have passed on. No one is truly ever gone, since all of us and our connections began at the Big Bang, the explosion of oneness into oneness, and have never come to an end. God asked Job, "Where were you when I laid the foundation of the earth?" (38:4). We might now respond, "We were with You." We say this boldly because "he chose us in Christ before the foundation of the world" (Eph 1:4).

We recall Teilhard's famous dictum: "Everything that rises must converge."[2] This further shows that evolution, as we saw above, is about more and more convergence, connection, and communion. Love is converging, connecting, and uniting, a tri-une oneness. This oneness also mirrors the interrelatedness of all material realities. To say that nothing stands alone but is linked to everything else is another way of affirming that love, the caring connection, is limitless.

To say that "God is love" is also a reference to the Trinity, since love always means a communion of relatedness. To say we are made in the image of God is to say we are made to be com-munitarian, as scientists and mystics tell us the whole universe is. Teilhard, the scientist and mystic, has helped us discover this splendid synthesis. In his essay "My Universe," he reminds us that "science alone cannot discover Christ. But Christ satisfies the yearnings that are born in our hearts in the school of science.... Science will, in all probability, be increasingly impregnated by mysticism."

Let's now explore the differences and similarities between science and mysticism. One difference is that science investigates the tangible things in the world by testing and retesting them for validation. A mystical state or intuition, since it is entirely expe-riential, is self-validating. Another is that scientific theory can be expressed in words. As we saw above, mystical realizations can-not be expressed in words. A scientific principle is confirmed by experimentation and repetition. A mystical experience may or may not be repeated. It is confirmed by its results; the mystic's experience leads him to show more love, have more wisdom, and act with more humility than ever before. This humility helps the world. In *Laudato Si'*, Pope Francis states, "Once we lose our humility, and become enthralled with the possibility of limitless mastery over everything, we inevitably end up harming society and the environment" (no. 224).

We see other differences: Science uses fact; mystics use paradox. Science is a form of knowledge; mysticism is a form of prayer. In Teilhard's view, these distinctions do not hold as trenchantly as we see them here. He appreciated science as a path to God, scientific truth as mystical truth, a unity we shall explore throughout this book.

We also see how science and mysticism resemble each other; both science and mystical theology say that we do not see things as they actually are. For instance, we can imagine that we are looking at the Rock of Gibraltar. The quantum physicist tells us that it looks solid and stationary but at a subatomic level it is actually spacious and moving. The ecologist tells us that the Rock looks separate, but is actually linked to everything in the world of nature around it. Thus, what we see with the naked, untrained eye does not reveal the full reality of what is there.

A mystic like Teilhard will say the same: Matter looks solid but it is transparent to spirit. All things seem to be just what they appear to be on the surface, but actually everything is ablaze with divine fire. In the Jungian view, fire represents the energy in the human psyche. For Teilhard, fire was a symbol of spiritual awakening and the transformative unity in all creation. Fire refers to love as an energy that can bring all things into oneness in Christ. Thus, what seems separate is linked. In the Sacred Heart of Jesus, we are all together in the renewing fire of love, the Holy Spirit of Pentecostal fire.

Let's return to the image of the Rock of Gibraltar. When a mystic says that God is in all things, she does not mean that there is an old man with a beard inside the Rock. She means what the physicists and ecologists mean: material reality is expansive, moving, connecting, and connected. In the mystical view, those are ways God is present in all of evolution. The divine-in-all does not refer to a separate supreme being in a rock or in any thing. It is the divine in matter because of what matter tells us: It is roomy enough to include what transcends it. It is connected and connecting so that love is its ultimate meaning, purpose, and goal. These are descriptions that also reflect what is meant by God.

The scientist knows that we do not perceive the full reality of things because our eyes are incapable of seeing the infinitesimal molecules that make them up. For the mystic, what we see with our eyes is also not the full picture. All things are actually transparent to the divine if we look with our soul. We can sense this capacity in Teilhard's phrase, "...ever more perfect eyes at the heart of a cosmos where there is always more to see" (PM, 31).

Teilhard's mystical spirituality is ultimately a celebration of God in the natural world, a hymn to the universe as the incarnate presence of God. In such vibrant vision, we experience unitive consciousness. This is not just a mental awareness but a bodily sense of the oneness that is God, ourselves, and all things.

Science has shown us that energy and matter are two aspects of one cosmic reality. The Big Bang, the big bursting forward, was the moment at which energy became matter. From then on, there has been a continuous exchange between them. Likewise, energy cannot be destroyed or ended. What we say of energy, we say of God: the divine life, that which does not end, is everywhere and everything. We see how science and mysticism can come to the same conclusion. All creation is energy reaching us in matter so that it can be seen. The logical mind does not grasp this, but a mystical intuitive like Teilhard did and we can too.

Teilhard also understood that there can be no division between human and divine, natural and supernatural, finite and infinite, mortal and immortal, sacred and profane, local and global, flesh and spirit, individual and collective, religion and science, creation and evolution. All these perennial oppositions can be seen as creative tensions when they unite and collaborate. Such unity of apparent opposites is the essence of a mystical perspective. We see this in Teilhard's essay "A Sketch of a Personalistic Universe," where he states, "There is neither spirit nor matter in the world; the stuff of the universe is *spirit-matter*....The physical structure of the universe is love [what makes two into one]."

Throughout the centuries, mystics have discerned three qualities in God: God is one; God is in all beings as what is loving them; and God is all "yes" to our human condition, so much so that God became one of us. To say that God is love is to say that love has the same three elements: love is unity consciousness rather than separation; love includes all beings rather than only our near and dear; and love is an unconditional "yes" to all that happens as opportunities to show our love.

Thus, when we experience oneness, show limitless love, and make a total surrender to reality, God is living in us not as an inhabitant but as the depth of our own being. Free of all dualism, we experience the mystical awareness of God as our true nature. Here are Teilhard's own words on these depths that a mystical consciousness takes us to:

> Beneath what is temporal and plural, the mystic can see only the unique Reality which is the support common to all substances, and which clothes and dyes itself in all the universe's countless shades without sharing their impermanence. He knows the joy of feeling that Reality penetrates all things—wherever the mysterious light of the Omnipresence had shone—even to the most hidden places of his own person—even into the very stuff of which his mental awareness, in the different forms it assumes, is made up. He soon comes to see the world as no more than the back-wash of one essential Thing whose pleasure it is to react upon itself, within the conscious minds it supports. To the mystic, everything is equally, and for ever, dear and precious....Now that I have found the transparent consistence in which we are all held, I realize that the mystical effort to see must

give way to the effort to feel and to surrender myself. This is the phase of communion. (WTW, 123)

Teilhard believed that the essential core of our humanity and of every planet in the cosmos is love, the divine life, creating, redeeming, and sanctifying all that is. Teilhard thus experienced the universe as having a heart—the Heart of Jesus, a heart on fire with zeal for the future of humanity, dedicated to cocreating with us a world of justice to end injustice, peace to end war, and love to end hate. Such a world displays the triumph of the risen Christ dispensing to us the graces of Easter.

1

GOD IN WORLD AND MATTER

To see a World in a Grain of Sand
And a Heaven in a Wild Flower
Hold Infinity in the palm of your hand
And Eternity in an hour....

—William Blake, "Auguries of Innocence"

In these four lines, the mystic poet William Blake shows us four main elements of nature mysticism. The first line states that the whole exists in every part. The next line cuts through any duality between heaven and earth. In the third line, we see how infinite space is present in the smallest place. Finally, we hear that infinite time is present in every hour and moment.

It is indeed easy to see the connection between mysticism and nature. Mysticism is about our union with God. The structure of nature reveals God's way of being united to us: nurturant like the earth, transcendent like the sky, dying and renewing like the seasons, the tides, and all that grows.

Teilhard, as a nature mystic, has the same vision: "Blessed be you, universal matter, immeasurable time, boundless ether, triple abyss of stars, atoms, and generations: you who by overflowing and dissolving our narrow standards or measurements reveal to us the dimensions of God" (HU, 66). We hear a similar strain from Rabbi Arthur Green:

> Understand the entire course of evolution, from the simplest life forms millions of years ago, to the great complexity of the human brain…and proceeding onward into the unknown future, to be a meaningful process. There is a One that is ever revealing itself to us within and behind the great diversity of life. That One is Being itself, the constant in the endlessly changing evolutionary parade.[1]

For Teilhard, earth also has an inner life. Matter always holds spirit, its interior life, divine aliveness, the *élan vital*, the evolutionary force that keeps everything going. Teilhard understood God to be this animating force in us and in all things, while nonetheless being personal. With nothing to go on but dualism, we might imagine God as a separate supreme Being above all beings. On the map of mystical consciousness, God is not a separate being but the Being of all that is. At the same time, God is relatable, personal to us, yet not someone else, somewhere else.

Thus, divine life incarnates, appears—and loves to appear—in nature and in us: "Heaven *and* earth are full of your glory." In the Bible, the word *glory* refers to divinity. This union of ourselves and God-in-nature awakens us to a reverence for and a love of earth and all beings. We find ourselves in a long spiritual lineage. For instance, our forefather in faith, Jacob, awoke to the recognition that the natural world was full of God's presence: "Then Jacob woke from his sleep and said, 'Surely the LORD is in this place—and I did not know it!' And he was afraid, and said, 'How awesome is this place! This is none other than the house of God, and this is the gate of heaven'" (Gen 28:16–17). Jacob summarized Teilhard's entire mysticism in one sentence! Teilhard himself noted this: "As Jacob said, awakening from his dream, the world, this palpable world, which we were wont to treat with the boredom and disrespect with which we habitually regard places with no sacred association for us, is in truth a holy place, and we did not know it" (DM).

This mystical perspective is not limited to the Judeo-Christian Tradition. We recall a similar reference to awakening to the power in matter in Buddha's words concerning enlightenment: "When the morning star appeared, I *and the great earth with all its beings* simultaneously became Buddhas [enlightened ones]." This is a way of affirming that there is no personal awakening without the whole world of matter—and all peoples—coming along with us. What it takes for any of us to awaken in the world is to include the world, to love the world. Then dualism ends and we see the divine *in* the world, not beside it or outside it. For Teilhard, the universe of matter is a theophany, that is, a reality translucent to the divine: "Ever since the creation of the world his eternal power and divine nature, invisible though they are, have been understood and seen through the things he has made" (Rom 1:20). We also see in this verse how our love for God is love for the world and all the people in it.

For Teilhard, all material things are birthing, living, dying, and rising in Christ. Incarnation means divinity in matter; Christ is the divine life in all matter. We find these encouraging cosmic realizations confirmed by St. Paul in Colossians: "He is the image of the invisible God, the firstborn of all creation; for in him all things in heaven and on earth were created, things visible and invisible, whether thrones or dominions or rulers or powers—all things have been created through him and for him. He himself is before all things, and in him all things hold together" (1:15–17; cf. 2:10, 3:11).

Thus, we live in God: "For 'In him we live and move and have our being'" (Acts 17:28). God is all around us in transcendence, within us in immanence. Likewise, God is the Beginning and the End, here from ancient hours, here in the present moment, ahead in future years: "'I am the Alpha and the Omega,' says the Lord God, who is and who was and who is to come, the Almighty" (Rev 1:8). We might also say "who is becoming." This same idea is reflected by Pope Francis:

> Everything is related, and we human beings are united as brothers and sisters on a wonderful pilgrimage, woven together by the love God has for each of his creatures and which also unites us in fond affection with brother sun, sister moon, brother river and mother earth. (*Laudato Si'* 92)

MEDITATION

For me, my God, all joy and all achievement, the very purpose of my being and all my love of life, all depend on this one basic vision of the union between yourself and the universe. Let others, fulfilling a function more august than mine, proclaim your splendors as pure Spirit; as for me, dominated as I am by a vocation which springs from the inmost fibers of my being, I have no desire, I have no ability, to proclaim anything except the innumerable prolongations of your incarnate Being in the world of matter; I can preach only the mystery of your flesh, you the Soul shining forth through all that surrounds us. (HU, 31)

Reflection

As you reflect on your life, you may realize how often we were locked into limiting beliefs and attitudes such as the following: "I believed there was a sharp line between my body and soul"; "I saw everything dualistically," or "My childhood was one, long distrust of my body, since I was taught that it was a vehicle for sin."

Then, finding the bigness of a cosmic faith,[2] a shift can occur in our perspective. Each of us then might say, "What a grace it has been to find the mystical path that has no fork in the road that makes me have to choose God over matter. The incarnation cancels out the old dualisms in favor of oneness. The union of matter and spirit that I glimpse in special moments of cosmic awareness makes me trust a divine life in, through, and around this one. I can see and feel the power of the incarnation, Christ in matter, when I look at anyone or anything. I can feel that all is suffused with Christ's life, that all that is has become *how* he lives here in my body, how he lives in all of me—and in everyone and everything."

Jesus prayed, "…that they may all be one. As you, Father, are in me and I am in you, may they also be in us, so that the world may believe that you have sent me. The glory that you have given me I have given them, so that they may be one, as we are one" (John 17:21–22). These references to "one," both among people and within the Trinity, are the oneness experienced in mysticism and in the cosmic spirituality of world and matter.

For Teilhard, all that we are and do is capable of divinization: "God truly waits for us in all things, unless indeed he advances to meet us" (DM, 16). These are two marvelous options. We can't miss meeting God, because we find God in the first instance or are found by God in the second. God awaits us in all natural things and in all that happens; God comes to meet us without waiting for us to make the first move.

In both options, we trust in grace. We notice that at times we have no choice. We find ourselves face-to-face with God in the things of nature, a life event, or a relationship. This happens when one or more trinitarian energies come through to us in what we see—creative, redemptive, loving. We feel that the world of matter and what is happening to us is part of God's *creative* process. We realize we were not created fully on the day of our birth; we are still being molded into wholeness. God does not give up on us. We then sense that the world and what is happening to us are objects of Christ's *redemptive* work. We realize we are still being redeemed, renewed, and liberated from the toils of ego-centeredness into the generosity of Christ's life in us. We feel that all we see and all that is happening to us is from *love*, for love, about love. We realize we are still loved and are learning to love in return by the grace of the Holy Spirit.

Both finding God and being found by God are evolutionary experiences. In the first, we gain mystical consciousness of the everywhere, everything that is God. In the second, we gain connection to the everywhere and everything that is God. Both pull back the curtain of dualism and show us heaven on earth, that is, the divine in matter.

In mystical intuition, we know that our human story, the story of the physical universe, cosmology, and the story in the Bible about God and us are meant to be one and the same. When we realize this, we find the union with God we always longed for. It is no different from the union with us that God has always longed for. And it all happens right here on the planet where there is only one story. It starts with the words "God so loved the world" (John 3:16).

Once we grasp the spectacular fact that material existence is permeated with the divine, even the most humdrum activity becomes a path to finding God. To say that the divine life pervades matter is, therefore, not only a comment on the cosmos. It is a comment on everything that happens or meets us in daily life.

The challenge is to recognize in the peeling of an avocado, in the opening of a window, in the writing of a note, that an animating force is in and with us. The phrase in *Star Wars*, "May the Force be with you," is not directed only to a larger-than-life hero with a galactic mission. The Force, God in matter, the energy and grace of the incarnation, is with us. We see it in every leaf and star; we hear it in every human voice that asks for our attention. Indeed, our attentiveness to the world and others is how the "Force," God—grace—can become present to others through us. In the spiritual life, nothing stops with us; all is meant to be shared: "As the Father has loved me, so I have loved you" (John 15:9).

God in the world and in matter means that all that we are and do, all that we feel and long for is how the creation, incarnation, redemption, and Pentecost are still happening everywhere around us. These are all events that happened at moments in time. Yet, each is sacramental in that graces are coming from them in the present—the same graces they beamed to humanity when they first occurred. This is why any *now* that opens to grace is sacramental. What a grace to be thankful for!

When the earth was thought to be flat, heaven was believed to be above us. Now that we know that the earth is round, we understand that heaven is indeed all around us.

> We do not believe that this earth is capable of
> becoming a new creation because we do not believe
> that this earthly creation, indeed the whole universe,
> is God-filled....Heaven is not a place of disembodied
> spirits but an embrace of love that transforms this
> present earthly life into the divine presence of
> enduring love. Heaven is this world clearly seen.
>
> —Ilia Delio, *Compassion*

Prayer

I see You in the morning dew and in the noontime sun.
I see You in the evening glow and in the starry night.
It is You I have been awed by in rainbows and rainstorms.
It is You I peer into when dawn and sundown show me
*   colors that defy my naming powers.*
I glimpse You growing in flowers, trees, and all green
*   things.*
I meet You moving through seasons.
It is You who is making every being in the world
*   translucent:*
If in the snow I were to look for You, I would peek at Your
*   countenance in the crystals, each one new, the You of so*
*   many faces.*
If in a mountain I were to look for You, I would already be
*   gazing at the outline of Your immortal body.*
May I keep meeting You without meeting, only uniting.
May I find You without finding, only feeling myself being
*   folded into Your Heart.*
May I embrace You without grasping, only lose myself in
*   Your arms that never stop holding me.*[3]

FOR FURTHER REFLECTION

All around us, to right and left, in front and behind, above and below, we have only to go a little beyond the frontier of sensible appearances in order to see the divine welling up and showing through. But it is not only close to us, in front of us, that the divine presence has revealed itself. It has sprung up universally, and we find ourselves so surrounded and transfixed by it, that there is no room left to fall down and adore it, even within ourselves. (DM, 83)

Christ invests himself organically with the very majesty of his creation. And it is in no way metaphorical to say that a human finds himself capable of experiencing and discovering his God in the whole length, breadth and depth of the world in movement. To be able to say literally to God that one loves him, not only with all one's body, all one's heart and all one's soul, but with every fiber of the unifying universe—that is a prayer that can only be made in space-time. (PM, 297)

By virtue of Creation, and still more the Incarnation, nothing here below is profane for those who know how to see. (DM, 30)

The truth is, indeed, that love is the threshold of another universe. Beyond the vibrations with which we are familiar, the rainbow-like range of its colors is still in full growth. But, for all the fascination that the lower shades have for us, it is only towards the "ultra" that the creation of light advances. It is in these invisible and, we might almost say, immaterial zones that we can look for true initiation into unity. *The depths we attribute to matter are no more than the reflection of the peaks of spirit.* (TF, 78)

Lord, since with every instinct of my being and through all the changing fortunes of my life, it is you whom I have ever sought, you whom I have set at the heart of universal matter, it will be in a resplendence which shines through all things and in which all things are, that I shall have the felicity of closing my eyes. (DM, xlvii)

Never say, "Matter is accursed, matter is evil" for there has come one who said...the words which spell my definitive liberation, "This is my body." Purity does not lie in separation from, but in a deeper penetration into the universe. It is to be found in the love of that unique, boundless Essence which penetrates the inmost depths of all things and there, from within those depths, deeper than the mortal zone where individuals and multitudes struggle, works upon them and molds them. Purity lies in a chaste contact with that which is "the same in all." Oh, the beauty of spirit as it rises up adorned with all the riches of the earth! (HU, 60, 64)

To Christify Matter: that sums up the whole venture of my innermost being. (HM, 47)

2

A SPIRITUALITY OF EVOLUTION

Creation has never stopped. The creative act is one huge continual gesture, drawn out over the totality of time…. The world is constantly emerging.

—Pierre Teilhard de Chardin,
Writings in Time of War

In Teilhard's view, each of us is coded to evolve continuously and ceaselessly. Indeed, each of us is evolution in person. Evolution refers to any process of formation and development. In biology, evolution refers to the continual changes in organisms over the course of centuries so they can adapt to the ever-shifting environment. The purpose of this evolution is survival. In social systems, evolution refers to gradual changes so that progress can occur. In individuals, evolution refers to the growth of our bodymind so that we can mature into a healthy adulthood. In spirituality, evolution refers to the step-by-step journey toward manifesting the wholeness that is in us.

For Teilhard, biological evolution is itself a spiritual event, since his theology is entirely incarnational. In Christ, the world

21

awakens to its divine essence and calling. Thus, evolution is a sacred process, not simply a scientific fact. Our vision of a cosmic Christ upholding and continuing the movement of evolution becomes clear in the Letter to the Hebrews: "He is the reflection of God's glory and the exact imprint of God's very being, and he sustains all things by his powerful word" (Heb 1:3).

As evolution moves toward greater complexity and greater consciousness, we also see a movement from matter to spirit. This does not mean that matter fades into something airy or abstract. Spirit completes matter and matter completes spirit. In the Buddhist *Heart Sutra*, we recall a similar realization: "Form is emptiness; emptiness is form." In this quotation, "emptiness" means being free of solidity and final definition, or in other words, openness to what continually unfolds. In the Christian view, what is unfolding is God's ongoing creation, the life of Jesus Christ in the history of humanity, the grace of the Holy Spirit in the evolution of the cosmos. Thus, in faith experience, evolution is a holy adventure.

An evolutionary spirituality always includes a love of our planet. We show this love by action for its welfare and against its depredation. We believe in the law of cause and effect; we acknowledge that many of our actions are harming our planet. We can't deny that our noxious emissions do not impact global warming. We can't fail to see the ecology being exploited. We can't help but notice the ongoing destruction of natural resources. We are fully aware that nuclear armaments threaten our planet's survival. An evolutionary spirituality includes a commitment to stand up for an end to these trends of death in favor of policies that support life. Once we have grasped that the cosmos is Christ's body, we understand that *caring about the ecology is the same as loving Jesus Christ*.

In addition, an awareness of how the earth, his body, is being damaged can become something we take personally. Pope Francis recommends such a response in *Laudato Si'*: "Our goal is…to dare to turn what is happening to the world into our own personal suffering and thus to discover what each of us can do about it" (no. 19).

Since everything in evolution is moving in the direction of consciousness and connection, those same impulses become central in an evolutionary spirituality. We are committed to grow in consciousness and to make caring connections. From a spiritual perspective, consciousness means wisdom and connection means love. "My love has grown over the decades and I feel wiser too," is a way of saying, "I am spiritually evolving."

It is comforting to trust that there is a loving intent in the universe. In evolutionary spirituality, we see that declaration as a call to show a loving intent in all we are and do. Since, in mystical consciousness, we are one with nature, then what drives her is meant to drive us too:

May all my choices have a loving intent.
May I act toward others and the world with a loving
    intent.
May my motives in all I do and am come from a
    loving intent.
May how I live my life be a way the universe shows its
    loving intent.

Holy Spirit, show me how what is happening to me today fits into my spiritual journey. What is Your loving intent in this? Show me where You want to take me.

MEDITATION

Since Jesus was born, and grew to his full stature, and died, everything has continued to move forward because Christ is not yet fully formed: he has not yet gathered about him the last folds of his robe of flesh

and of love which is made up of his faithful follow-
ers. The mystical Christ has not yet attained to his full
growth; and therefore the same is true of the cosmic
Christ. Both of these are simultaneously in the state of
being and of becoming; and it is from the prolongation
of this process of becoming that all created activity ultimately springs. Christ is the end point of the evolution,
even the natural evolution, of all beings; and therefore
evolution is holy. (HU, 58)

Reflection

We are not only aging because time is passing. Time is giving us an opportunity to advance into the image we were born to
reflect, that of Jesus Christ. He wants to gather us, our body, our
love, and our faith as the "folds of his robe of flesh and of love."
This makes every expression of our love the real presence of the
body of Christ on earth.

We look over the decades of our life and realize they have not
been perfect. We have regrets about some of our choices, about
opportunities we missed, missteps we took, mistakes we made,
and going too far or not far enough. Yet none of that disqualifies
us from our journey to a likeness to Jesus. We can continue on the
path from wherever we came from, as whoever we are now. What
has gone before, no matter how damaged or dissolute, has not
ruined our chances to fulfill our destiny. This is because *nothing
about our life so far has cancelled out God's love for us.* Christ is trying
harder than we are to attain "his full growth" in us. Our faith challenge is trusting in that. Wisdom and love may follow by grace.

Yet, wisdom and love in us do not always proceed in an
upward motion. They seem to go through seasons, sometimes
springing up, sometimes wintering down. As we reflect on our
life and its many cycles, we come to understand that the evolving
seasons of the year have a meaning beyond the merely biological.

They are a metaphor for how our life evolves from spring bud to summer bloom, from fall down to winter death and then to spring life again. We recall the words of Shakespeare: "Even through the hollow eyes of death I spy life peering."[1]

We can feel ourselves both being and becoming like everything that exists in nature. What happens in the entire cosmos happens in each of us; we are fully ourselves *and* still becoming ourselves each day. The "ourselves" is the risen Christ, what we look like in his mirror, our full identity in the spiritual world, the essence of holiness.

We can let go of believing that holiness is too much to aim for in our spiritual life. We can cease thinking that holiness only applies to the saints of old. Now we see how we can be involved in the holy venture of commitment to evolving in goodness, gentleness, and love. That commitment to continually evolving is holiness even without full accomplishment of it. Evolution in science describes how life works. Evolutionary spirituality is how our inner life works.

Nothing can sever the seamless robe of Christ's flesh, this cosmos. We belong here and it is a joy to be here because salvation, wholeness, and holiness happen here. Our role is to do all it takes to build a bodymind of psychological and spiritual wholeness. Our psychological work is clear to us nowadays in the recommendations of therapy and the self-help movement. Our spiritual work is outlined in the Scriptures and in the words and practices of teachers and mystics from a variety of traditions. We also find our path by pondering our experiences, longings, needs, aspirations, relationships, and life events. In each of them, we can find opportunities for Christ-like presence in the world. That presence can incarnate itself in daily specific acts of loving-kindness toward everyone we meet and in social action for the welfare of the world.

The most important ingredient in holiness is grace, the free offer to us of divine support. We will find this grace in all we encounter from people and events on the path itself. Our cosmic spirituality will also show us how grace can come to us in nature, so pregnant with divine life. All we have to say is yes to these ever-evolving gifts.

Evolution is the ongoing transformation of the impulse to live into the will to love. An evolutionary spirituality is about making the same transition in our personal lives.

End in what All begins and ends in: Yes!

—*The Rubáyát of Omar Khayyám*,
translated by Edward Fitzgerald

Prayer

May I open to more and more consciousness, more and more connection.

May I keep evolving in bodily wholesomeness so that I can offer robust service to people and to the planet.

May I keep evolving in mind and imagination so I can find ever new ways to see God in the cosmos.

May I keep evolving in personality until I let go of ego-centeredness in favor of world consciousness.

May I keep evolving in my relationships so I can show the same love to others that Christ shows to his Church.

May my heart keep evolving until I let go of narrow and selective loving in favor of universal and unconditional loving-kindness.

May I keep evolving in loving intent toward all beings as I abide in Christ and Christ in me.

May I keep asking what the Holy Spirit wants from me and opening myself to the grace to practice it.

FOR FURTHER REFLECTION

If humanity is to use its new access of physical power with balanced control, it cannot do so without a rebound of intensity in its zest to act, in its zest to seek, in its zest to create. (HM, 97)

God is at work in life. He helps it, raises it up, gives it the impulse that drives it along...in the current of living events that make the world of today. (WTW, 159)

The offering you really want, the offering you mysteriously need every day to appease your hunger, to slake your thirst, is nothing less than the growth of the world borne ever onwards in the stream of universal becoming. (HU, 12)

Evolution is a light illuminating all facts, a curve that all lines must follow....The consciousness of each of us is evolution looking at itself and reflecting upon itself....Man is not the center of the universe as once we thought in our simplicity, but something much more wonderful—the arrow pointing the way to the final unification of the world. (PM, 218)

Man is not yet complete in Nature, that is, he is not fully created—but that, in and around us, he is still in the full swing of evolution. (SC, 200)

The keystone of the arch which we must build is in our hands. To affect the synthesis between faith in God and faith in the world which our generation awaits, nothing would be better than to dogmatically define the cosmic aspect and function of the presence of Christ which makes him organically the author and director, the soul of evolution. (CE, 180)

The great cosmic attributes of Christ, those which (particularly in St John and St Paul) accord him a universal and final primacy over creation, these attributes...only assume their full dimension in the setting of an evolution...that is both spiritual and convergent. (SC, 189)

3

LOVE AND LOVING

How can we fail to be struck by the revealing growth
around us of a strong mystical current, actually nourished
by the conviction that the universe, viewed in its complete
workings, is ultimately lovable and loving.

—Teilhard de Chardin, *The Appearance of Man*

This world and its ecology survive by continually interacting
and interlinking. This is also how we can design our life
and spiritual practices. Love is an ongoing linking, an enduring
and caring connection. This relatedness moves in three directions:
toward ourselves, toward those with whom we are in relationships,
and toward all beings.

We can connect to ourselves in a caring way. This will include
self-nurturance and self-protection. Physically, we take care of our
bodies and avoid what might harm our health or spirit. Psychologically, we do what helps us grow in self-esteem. We want an
ego that is assertive but not aggressive, self-advocating, and not
passive.

In our relationships to our family, our friends, and to a part-
ner, we act with integrity and loving-kindness. We are respectful
of others' deepest needs, values, and wishes. We show attention,

acceptance, appreciation, affection, allowance. We ask the same from them. We keep our agreements and work out conflicts. This is how connection becomes commitment.

Our caring connection can extend to the world around us and to all the people in it, neutral, known, unknown, liked, and disliked. Indeed, in cosmic consciousness, the word *us* has no limit to what it includes. We hear how this happens in psychological terms from Carl Jung: "This widened consciousness...is bringing the individual into an absolute, binding, and indissoluble communion with the world at large."[1]

In ethical terms, we care about "the world at large," our planet, by refusing to engage in what might harm it. We oppose biocide (killing of living systems) and geocide (killing of earth resources by pollution). Positive actions include replacing the paradigm of domination and ownership of the earth with that of communing with and sharing the earth. Likewise, we treat the earth as a living being rather than a residence for beings. Then all beings exist in a single alive being, the mystical body of Christ, this cosmos of oneness. James Finley writes in *The Awakening Call*, "The universe is God's body in that it embodies the reality of his love which alone truly is and without which nothing is."[2] Indeed, if all is linked, then love is all there is.

Love is the source of our being, its goal, its purpose. Love is energy, a way of being fully present in the here and now in accord with what the vast web of life is up to: thriving by interrelatedness. Teilhard shows his appreciation of this touching fact when he writes, "Love is the most universal, the most tremendous and the most mysterious of cosmic forces. Love is the primal and universal psychic energy. Love is a sacred reserve of energy; it is like the blood of spiritual evolution."[3]

In the Gospels, God the Father speaks only twice, using many of the same words: "This is my Son, the Beloved, with whom I am well pleased" (Matt 3:17; 17:5). In both instances, God's words are about love. By grace, the one in whom he is pleased includes

Jesus, us, and this cosmos. "Pleased" refers to love. God is love toward Christ, us, and all that is. Hearts like ours, so limitless in extent, can't be satisfied until we have as much love for all beings as God has for us.

In the Gospel of Thomas, we read, "The light in a person of light lights up the whole world." Aristotle, and later St. Thomas Aquinas, declared that it is in the nature of goodness to spread itself around. We let that happen when we show goodness to others as God does to us. Indeed, God has been doing that since the Big Bang, the great diffusing of divine goodness. The Good became all the things that exist so it could spread out in every direction. The Hindu mystic Sri Aurobindo expressed this same mystical idea in *Thoughts and Glimpses*: "What, you ask, was the beginning of it all? Existence multiplied itself for sheer delight of being. It plunged into numberless trillions of forms so that it might find itself innumerably."[4]

Both the *Baltimore Catechism* and the new *Catechism of the Catholic Church* say that we are here to know, love, and serve God:

- To know love is to know God.
- To love ourselves, others, and the cosmos is to love God.
- To serve God is to serve humanity and care for the earth with loving-kindness and a commitment to global concerns.

All three of these are our callings and are what we are actually responding to when we pray, "Thy kingdom come." Our commitments to earth and people are our contribution to fulfilling our prayer.

No one can fully comprehend the uncreated God with his knowledge; but each one, in a different way, can grasp him fully through love. Truly this is the unending miracle of love: that one loving person, through his love, can embrace God, whose being fills and transcends the entire creation.[5]

MEDITATION

Love alone is capable of uniting living beings in such a way as to complete and fulfill them, for it alone takes them and joins them by what is deepest in themselves.... A universal love is not only psychologically possible; it is the only complete and final way in which we are able to love....Driven by the forces of love, the fragments of the world seek each other so that the world may come into being. (PM, 264–67)

Reflection

How do we feel divine love in us? We feel it in moments of grace. We feel divine love in us when we are being stirred to act lovingly, especially toward people beyond our limited circle of affection. We feel God's love moving us when we become mediators of healing and reconciliation in society, transcending the limits of our Cro-Magnon ancestry that tell us to retaliate and divide. We feel Christ's love in us when we are moved to go beyond the limits imposed by ego-centeredness. Teilhard wrote, "Union with Christ...implies the radical sacrifice of egoism" (DM, 61).

The common thread is the line from what is limited in us, ego, to what is limitless about us, God within. Life, in all its vicissitudes and challenges, offers us a thread that can lead us out of the labyrinth of ego. We present ourselves best on this holy path when we ask for the grace to be opened, unfolded, connected, restored, completed, accompanied, and guided. We surrender to what opens us. Our surrender is yes to the Holy Spirit. In actuality, we are hearing the Holy Spirit saying yes in us.

There is a powerful connection between yes and love. How? We have the capacity to say yes, to surrender to this moment in whatever shape it takes. Our surrender to what is really happening is to love what is. With every yes, we feel an enlargement of our capacity to relate to reality directly and fearlessly. This is the grace of the indwelling Spirit giving us the courage to show our love limitlessly.

This lifespan of ours is Christ's opportunity to walk the earth again and show love to all beings of this day and age. Our challenge is to shift from self-centeredness to selfless love, what God is. In the mystical view, our limitation in time and space is how we are other than God. Our moments of limitless loving are ways we live God's life on earth, our incarnational calling. We recall St. Athanasius: "For the Son of God became man so that we might become God."[6]

Indeed, no matter what we have done or how we are wounded, we are and remain deep down an incarnation of Christ's consciousness, our true self, yet another name for the limitless love that is God. Thomas Merton wrote, "God Himself…begins to live in me not only as my Creator but as my other and true self."[7]

We may love others in proportion to how lovable they are to us. Yet, our faith that God is love means that our loving no longer has limits, conditions, prerequisites, qualifications, or preferences in how it disperses itself. We love because we are love. We show love to everyone because there are no credentials they need before we choose to do so. We have broken our tie to selectiveness; all are included, another bow to oneness. The true self, beyond birth and death, has always had that aptitude to show love, *agape*, with no endpoint in sight. Richard Rohr notes, "Like Jesus, we are to love others not because of who *they* are, but because of who *we* are—all and equally the beloved of God."[8]

This is a radical way of looking at love because it overturns our natural inclination to move toward what attracts us and away from what repulses us. In Buddhism, being tied to either of these inclinations is the central cause of suffering. The alternative, the antidote to suffering, is letting go of clinging or running, then opening to universal and unconditional loving-kindness. The move of evolution toward more and more connectivity becomes not only what moves the worlds but what moves us. This is an example of the evolutionary spirituality of Teilhard in action: "Mankind will only find and shape itself if people can learn to love one another in the very act of drawing closer" (FM, 233).

Our lives are composed of five concentric circles of connection with other humans: We are in the first innermost circle. The circle around ours includes those close to us, those we love and care about. Next is the circle of neutral people, those with whom we are acquainted or toward whom we are indifferent. Toward them we are courteous, compassionate, or at least nonharming. The challenging next one holds those we want to avoid, can't stand, don't like, enemies, anyone with whom we have difficulties. The outermost circle includes all beings everywhere, people we will never meet or ever know:

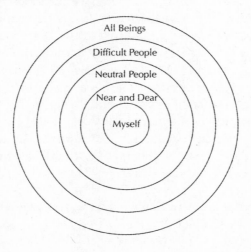

We all exist in the same set of circles. Our love is often limited to ourselves and those we love. We don't go beyond those two circles. In the practice of divine loving-kindness, our love expands so that we, daily and consciously, beam love to all the members of all the circles—just what Jesus is doing right now. We do not show our love to all in the same way, but our love extends to them all nonetheless. Our universal love is energy from the God-as-love inside us. Teilhard says, "The only subject ultimately capable of mystical transfiguration is the whole of humankind forming a single body and a single soul in love" (DM, 121). Thus, our love is meant to embrace all beings in all our circles of connection. This lofty spiritual generosity is a sign of the Heart of Jesus beating in us as the motivating force of our life.

Most of us no longer believe in an interventionist God, a feature of dualism. Once we really comprehend that God is love, it is up to us to show the love that is God in our actions and interventions in the world. Our spiritual practice of active love in the world means that we stay on the lookout for injustice anywhere it appears and open our heart to the suffering it causes. We then show courage under fire, taking a stand for fairness, speaking truth to power, letting the light through no matter how dark the world becomes. Teilhard suggests, "Do not brace yourself against suffering. Try to close your eyes and surrender yourself, as if to a great loving energy" (OS, 112). This love-energy is God acting in us. The God who is love can intervene, but only through us. We recall the story of the bombed-out cathedral in a German town toward the end of World War II. A statue of Jesus showing his Heart had fallen over. It was intact except it had no hands. Once the statue was put into a standing position, an American G.I. placed a note at its base: "I have no hands but yours."

Everything that is hurt, everything that seemed to us dark, harsh, shameful, maimed, ugly, irreparably damaged, is in

Christ transformed and recognized as whole, as lovely, and radiant in Light. We awaken as the Beloved in every last part of our body.

—St. Symeon, *Hymns of Divine Love*, 15

Prayer

God who is love, give me the grace to show the love You are in all that I am, think, feel, and do.
Let me then be an emissary of light when darkness surrounds me and others.
Let me bear witness to enduring hope in despair, both my own and that of others.
Let me show loving-kindness no matter what others may do.
Free my heart from its inclination to hurt or retaliate.
Give me the courage to speak truth to power, especially when I am afraid to do so.
Help me grow in caring concern for people and the planet.
May I show all the love I have in any way I can here, now, and all the time, to everything and everyone—including me—since love is what I am and why I'm here.
Now nothing matters to me more or gives me greater joy.
Thank you for the grace that opened my heart to Your loving way.

FOR FURTHER REFLECTION

No work is more effective or brings greater peace than to gather together, in order to soothe it and offer it to God, the suffering of the world….No attitude allows the soul to expand more freely, than to open itself, generously and tenderly—with and in Christ—to sympathize with all suffering…cosmic compassion. (OS, 6)

Charity does more than call on us to bind up wounds: it urges us to build a better world here below, and to be in the forefront of every attack launched to forward the growth of mankind....And personal salvation is important not so much because it will bring about our own beatification as because it makes us effect in ourselves the salvation of the world. (SC, 123)

The hidden existence and eventual release of forces of attraction between people...are as powerful in their own way as nuclear energy appears to be. (FM, 233)

To love is to discover and complete oneself in someone other than oneself, an act impossible of general realization on Earth so long as each can see in the neighbor no more than a closed fragment following its own course through the world. It is precisely this state of isolation that will end if we begin to discover in each other not merely the elements of one and the same thing, but of a single Spirit in search of Itself. (FM, 84)

One by one, Lord, I see and I love all those whom you have given me to sustain and charm my life. One by one also I number all those who make up that other beloved family which has gradually surrounded me, its unity fashioned out of the most disparate elements, with affinities of the heart, of scientific research and of thought. And again one by one—more vaguely it is true, yet all-inclusively—I call before me the whole vast anonymous army of living humanity; those who surround me and support me though I do not know them; those who come, and those who go; above all, those who in office, laboratory and factory, through their vision of truth or despite their error, truly believe in the progress of earthly reality and who today will take up again their impassioned pursuit of the light. (HU, 12)

Suffering can be transformed into an expression of love and a principle of union. Yes: suffering itself, obscure and ugly, elevated... into a supremely active principle of universal humanization and divinization. (OS, 118)

4

OUR INNER DEPTHS

*The light will emerge only when we go deeper. We shall
see its radiance only if we leave behind the outer husk
of beings and succeed in discovering what is hidden deep
down in them.*

—Pierre Teilhard de Chardin, *Science and Christ*

Such depths in us, such an incomprehensible identity beyond
our "outer husk" of ego must have a purpose in the psyche.
That purpose is finding God within, what hitches us to everything
else until there is no "else." When we say God is transcendent, we
mean that what God transcends is dualism, otherness.

It is a theological dictum that we can't comprehend the mystery of God. This realization also implies that we can't fully know
ourselves since in our core we are what God is. Speaking for myself,
*I am something deeper than I will ever fully experience. I have only a
hint about who I am. All these years of "knowing myself" have given me
barely a sixth-grade competency in the geography of my soul. Who I am
will always be bigger than my capacity for knowing who I am.*

St. Francis asked, "God who are you? God, who am I?" It takes
only one answer to address both halves of his question. In mystical

awareness, God is the real "Who" in "Who am I?" In mystical consciousness, the more we know ourselves, the more we know God and vice versa. So Plato's imperative "Know yourself" turns out to be a deeply spiritual recommendation. Likewise, since God, we, and all that is exist in oneness, "whoever has known himself has simultaneously come to know the depth of all things."[1]

The phrase "God within" shows clearly that we can't know all about the within of ourselves. We intuit that there is something that knows us but that we can't know. At the same time, in mystical consciousness, we feel no more need to know anyway. St. John of the Cross, in his poem "Entreme Donde No Supe," states it well:

> I entered I knew not where,
> And there I stood not knowing:
> Nothing left to know.

Nonetheless, Teilhard, in "Private Notes," reminds us of God's longing to communicate with us: "A presence is never mute." The divine is audible not as a voice of someone standing in a room with us. Divine presence is more like the roominess of the infinite in both of us and in all that is. It is roomy because no rigid certitudes or demand for logic are in the way.

How does our inner life reveal God's life in us? St. Thomas says that beings remain in being by what they do. Thus, a maple tree continues in being by growing as the maple tree it is. A human goes on being human by human thought and behavior. However, God remains in being as being itself; God is because he is himself. So living in the image of God happens in us precisely when we are simply being who we are—*When I am most I, I am most like God*. Mystic St. Catherine of Genoa exclaimed, "My being is God, not by simple participation only but by a true transformation. I say: my *self* is God, nor is any other self known to me except my God."[2] "Be still, and know that I am God!" (Ps 46:10) is thus: "Be still and know that I am your I am." We recall the Gnostic teacher

Allogenes: "There was within me a stillness of silence, and I heard the Blessedness whereby I knew my proper self."[3] Our longing for God is a longing for soul, the essence of ourselves, our true nature.

We can't come to such mystical consciousness on our own. What holy irony—we can't find our highest identity, what is best in us, our true self, on our own. We need union with God to know ourselves, a gift of grace.

The religious question is primarily a question of life, of living or not living in the higher union which opens itself to us as a gift.

—William James, *The Varieties of Religious Experience*

MEDITATION

For the first time in my life perhaps, I took the lamp and, leaving the zone of everyday occupations and relationships where everything seems clear, I went down into my inmost self, to the deep abyss whence I feel dimly that my power of action emanates. But as I moved further and further away from the conventional certainties by which social life is superficially illuminated, I became aware that I was losing contact with myself. At each step of the descent a new person was disclosed within me of whose name I was no longer sure, and who no longer obeyed me. And when I had to stop my exploration because the path faded beneath my steps, I found a bottomless abyss at my feet, and out of it comes—arising I know not from where—the current which I dare to call *my* life. (DM, 42)

Reflection

We might look into ourselves using words like these: "I think I know myself. This knowledge refers to the obvious characteristics in my personality, my traits, my body, my skills, my knowledge, my wishes, my needs, my values, my history, my conflicts, and all the information on my driver's license. But what happens when I am asleep, and in my dreams I see parts of me that shock, surprise, and sometimes alarm me? In my unconscious life, I am meeting up with another self altogether. Likewise, in moments of deep reverie or reflection, I see capacities and limitations that are not so apparent in the ordinary light of day. In other words, there is a day version of me that follows conventions and has clarity. There is also a night or reverie version of me that continually shifts from conscious to unconscious."

Teilhard is saying that, as he "moved further and further away from the conventional certainties" of the superficial world, he lost contact with his usual sense of himself. We might hear ourselves respond,

"I sometimes live life on the surface, concerned with convention and with maintaining a social image. When that happens, I lose track of the nighttime me, the deeper reaches of myself that surface mysteriously at special times. St. John of the Cross says that in the darkest night we meet the God who is love. Am I losing my chance for an encounter with the Beloved when I make choices that keep me tied to superficialities and banalities?

"I want to contact and commune with the true reality of who I am, the one with no name I can make out, the one who does not obey the rules that keep me safe from surprise; the one who has no clear path; the one who has no ground because he is falling into a void that has no bottom. There and only there will I find the real me.

"I will finally grasp that I have no separate self. I am a single articulation of the oneness of all that is. In that empowering realization, I will hear Jesus inviting me to see all that I am, both conscious and unconscious, both artificial and authentic, both shallow and deep, as totally acceptable to him. He sees me not in parts but as one in myself and one with all beings, all one in him. I am an answer to his prayer that all be one.

"I find my true identity not only by what psychology suggests, higher self-esteem and more self-awareness. I find my identity when I show up with Jesus to end prejudice, hate, greed, aggression, and division in my own life and in the world. This spirituality of Jesus takes me beyond what psychology can tell me about me. With this spiritual commitment, I already know what I will look like. My face will be that of Jesus Christ, my heart his."

Experiences in childhood, school, church, society, and among peers may have damaged our sense of self. Our self-esteem is low; our trust in an interior treasury of wisdom is hard to maintain. We usually think of our woundedness as a psychological problem only. As we look into our deficit more deeply, we realize that it is a spiritual malady as well. We have been locked out of our own interior castle, where a treasury of spiritual practices and powers has been stored for us. We do not overlook or deny our need for therapy or for the psychological tools that can help us. We make full use of them. But we can also increase our conscious contact with Christ. We can turn to a solid spiritual director and to spiritual practices for help. We can ask for grace.

We can best access our inner spiritual resources as we stay in communion with the indwelling Spirit. We begin to notice intuitions and realizations that point us to what comes next on our path, to what works and what does not work for our spiritual evolution. Most of all, we begin to expand our ken so that it includes a planetary consciousness, a sure sign of the Holy Spirit alive in us.

It all begins with exploring the mystery of God and ourselves: "I found...the current which I dare to call my life" (DM, 42).

Prayer (Based on Psalm 139)

You have looked deeply into me, and You know me through
    and through.
You know my every move.
You pick up on my thoughts from afar.
You know all my little ways.
Before I say a word You know what I will say.
In all this, You know me not as a spy but as a lover who
    supports and holds me.
I feel Your hand in mine even now.
These realizations are too deep for me to grasp fully, too
    lofty for me to comprehend.
Where could I go if I wanted to get away from You?
If I were to go to heaven, You would be there
    welcoming me.
If I were to go deep into the earth, You would be waiting
    for me there too.
If I were to get up with the sun and then find a way to
    settle at the far side of the sea,
      it would be Your hand that had led me all along, only
        You holding me.
Were I to hide in the cloak of night, that kind of darkness
    would be daylight to You.
For You are the loving author of all of me, known and
    unknown by me.
I praise and thank You for how wonderfully You made me.
All Your works in the entire cosmos are made in the same
    wonder-filled way.
I was made in the world and of what the world is made.
You saw my body before I was conceived and already
    loved me.
You knew how many days I would have here, even before
    they began.

*The contemplations of Your Heart are precious to me. So
vast a sum, too many to count.
When I sleep, You are my dreams. When I awake, I am
still with You.*

FOR FURTHER REFLECTION

The work of works for humans is to establish, in and by means
of each of us, an absolutely original center in which the universe
reflects itself in a unique and inimitable way. (PM, 261)

Let us establish ourselves in the divine milieu. There we shall find
ourselves where the soul is most deep and matter is most dense.
There we shall discover with the confluence of all beauties, the
ultra-vital, the ultra-sensitive, the ultra-active point of the universe. And at the same time we shall feel the plenitude of our powers of action and adoration effortlessly ordered within our deepest
selves....The greater man becomes, the more humanity becomes
united with the consciousness of and mastery of its potentialities,
the more beautiful creation will be, the more perfect adoration
will become. Then Christ will find, for mystical extensions, a body
worthy of resurrection. (DM, 133)

Lord, lock me up in the deepest depths of your heart; and then,
holding me there, burn me, purify me, set me on fire, sublimate
me, till I become utterly what you would have me be, through the
utter annihilation of my ego. (HU, 26)

The death of egoism is to understand that one is an element in a
universe that personalizes itself by uniting itself with God. So it is
no longer oneself that one loves in oneself. (OS, 55)

My God, I deliver myself up with utter abandon to those fear-
ful forces of dissolution which, I blindly believe, will this day
cause my narrow ego to be replaced by your divine presence.
(HU, 25)

This crumbling away, which is the mark of the corruptible and the precarious, is to be seen everywhere. And yet everywhere there are traces of, and a yearning for, a unique support, a unique and absolute soul, a unique reality in which other realities are brought together in synthesis, as stable and universal as matter, as simple as spirit….Having come face to face with a universal and enduring reality…a glorious unsuspected feeling of joy invaded my soul. (HU, 98)

The inner face of the world is manifest deep within our human consciousness. (PM, 63)

5

THE COSMIC CHRIST

If I knew how to immerse myself in him [Christ], if I knew how to implant myself in him, I would find in myself the Love that fills him.

—Pope St. John Paul II, "Reflections on Fatherhood"

Teilhard affirms the place of Christ in the cosmos in his essay "Cosmic Life" in *Writings in Time of War*: "Christ has a cosmic body that extends throughout the universe." Thus, the entire cosmos is the mystical body of Christ. This stupendous fact is about us too: "To live the cosmic life is to live dominated by the consciousness that one is an atom in the body of the mystical and cosmic Christ. The man who so lives dismisses as irrelevant a host of preoccupations that absorb the interest of other men: his life is projected further, and his heart more widely receptive" (WTW, 70).

Teilhard, in a letter to Andre Ravier, SJ, saw that Christ's humanity included both "a terrestrial nature and a cosmic nature." The phrase "cosmic Christ" refers to this combination. First, Jesus walked on the earth as one who loved it: "Having loved his own who were in the world, he loved them to the end" (John 13:1). Second, Christ stands in the cosmos as the pioneer of its evolution into spiritual consciousness. This is because the cosmos was, and is still being created through him: "All things came into being through him" (John 1:3). Likewise, Christ embraces and suffuses all that is: "the fullness of him who fills all in all" (Eph 1:23).

We have a cosmic identity, calling, and destiny; we are here to join in Christ's eternal yes to the evolving of our planet. We do this by more and more caring and compassionate connectedness, that is, more and more love. We show this love by a zealous concern for the earth and all beings on it. When I have a faith big enough to trust this love burning within me, I will, as Pope John Paul said, *"find in myself the Love that fills him."* In mystical awareness, we can see this as another way of saying that what Christ is we are. We hear Gerard Manley Hopkins echo this:

> In a flash, at a trumpet crash,
> I am all at once what Christ is, since he was what I
>   am.[1]

The Christ who is the origin, model, and goal of evolution is more than the Christ of a particular religion. This is the cosmic Christ of universal consciousness transcending individuality. He calls us to the same freedom from separateness. What about this cosmic consciousness and connectedness in the life of Jesus?

In the first days of his life, Jesus was circumcised and became a "child of Abraham." Yet, as an adult, we hear him describe himself this way: "Very truly, I tell you, before Abraham was, I am" (John 8:58). Here we meet the cosmic Christ, transcending the tribal religious affiliation of his childhood in favor of universal consciousness. When he shows love for all people, Jew and Gentile alike, Jesus transcends sectarian connection in favor of universal connectedness: "Christ is all and in all!" (Col 3:11). Likewise, Teilhard says, "Jesus must be loved as a world" (WTW, 148).

Christ invites us to the same realization about ourselves. In our true nature, we are universal consciousness and universal connectedness. Both of these are exactly what progress in evolution. Here "there is no longer Greek and Jew, circumcised and uncircumcised, barbarian, Scythian, slave and free" (Col 3:11).

Here is another example of the transition from a tie to a single belief system to a universal awareness. As a faithful Jew, Jesus surely prayed Psalm 23: "The LORD is my shepherd." Yet we notice what he says in full self-revelation: "I am the good shepherd" (John 10:11). Again we see the difference between separate and universal identity. The Christ referred to in Teilhard's evolutionary view is nothing less than *cosmic Christ consciousness and connectedness*. In mystical, nondual awareness, the "I am" statements in John's Gospel reveal not only who Christ is but who we are too.

The very first sentence of that Gospel introduces Christ as the eternal Word from the beginning, the mystical God-Human, preexisting history or religious denomination, pantraditional not sectarian, cosmic not partisan, a universal not a discrete consciousness. In John 10:30, Jesus speaks of this divine consciousness directly: "The Father and I are one." When that verse is used only to prove he is God, we miss the many-splendored implications that arise in mystical consciousness; Jesus is continually showing us the oneness he and we are: "There is no longer Jew or Greek, there is no longer slave or free, there is no longer male and female; *for all of you are one in Christ Jesus*" (Gal 3:28 , emphasis added).

To say there is a cosmic Christ is to break open the narrow confines that might make our faith too small. We can instead think big about what is possible in the world. We can trust how well-equipped we are to care for and repair it since we are made in the image of Christ the Divine Architect and Redeemer of the universe.

In the bigness of the cosmic Christ, we are emancipated from a constricting nationalism and brought into citizenry in a global kingdom. The kingdom of Christ is not based on a dominance model but on an all-inclusive model. We are here as planetary-conscious beings, incarnate for a lifetime, en route to a resurrection for all time. Oneness in this context is not only about nonduality. It is about our day-by-day commitment to join into the incarnation and resurrection events of Jesus Christ, cosmic in extent.

The Heart of the cosmic Christ is larger in scope and promise than we have seen in any traditional image with which we are familiar. There is no frame around this image of the loving Heart, only endless rays that reach into the hundred million galaxies that surround us. The cosmic Christ is the image in which we were made, what we already are but still find so hard to believe or express. Yet, the cosmic Christ is also a source of grace sufficient for the task. We keep seeing this grace coming toward us in every living thing, in every time and place, in every event, in every comfort, in every challenge. All we have to say is yes.

MEDITATION

By virtue of Christ's rising again, nothing any longer kills inevitably, but everything is capable of becoming the blessed touch of divine hands, the blessed influence of the will of God upon our lives. However marred by our faults or however desperate our circumstances may be, we can, by a total reordering, completely correct the world that surrounds us and resume our lives in a favorable way. "For those who love God everything can be transformed into good." This is the fact which dominates all explanation and discussion. (DM, 49)

Reflection

The cosmic Christ is the eternal and risen Christ. The resurrection is not simply a proof that Christ is alive or that our religion is true. The resurrection is ongoing and opens us to mystical realizations about ourselves and our world. Animated by faith, we hear ourselves say, "The risen Christ is alive in every here and now of my life. In every event and feeling, in this moment or in any, I meet the risen Christ. This becomes clear when I find in this moment an opening to affirm life, show love, and trust the power of grace."

Resurrection makes our contact with God real. The risen Christ is the Christ we receive in the Eucharist, the Christ we adore, the Christ we imitate, the Christ who loves us individually, the Christ whose body is the cosmos, the Christ we turn to, and the Christ who gives us the graces to cocreate with him a new kingdom on earth of heavenly design.

At an archetypal level, resurrection symbolizes that death is not an ending of life only part of the cycle of continual renewal. The resurrection of Christ is what gives us hope that injustice, death, and hate will not have the final word in our human story. As Teilhard states, "Nothing any longer kills inevitably." *Our hope persists not because injustices will finally end but because they are not final.* Teilhard comments, "We must overcome death by finding God in it. And by the same token, we shall find the divine established in our innermost hearts, in the last stronghold which might have seemed able to escape his reach….Christ has conquered death, not only by suppressing its evil effects, but by reversing its sting" (DM, 49).

Just as matter cannot be destroyed, only transformed, likewise, everything about us humans has a capacity for transformation. Believing that can happen is faith in the power of Christ's resurrection in our lives. "By virtue of Christ's rising again…the blessed influence of the will of God upon our lives….": in these phrases, Teilhard connects resurrection with the will of God, reality, the givens of life we are here to accept with an unconditional yes. Givens of life are beyond our control to alter or erase. The things we cannot change are then not simply facts. They are the components of God's will. At the incarnation, Jesus entered into and said yes to the givens of life on this planet. That was how he combined his cosmic nature and his lowly humility.

St. Irenaeus wrote that Christ "did not despise or evade any condition of humanity, nor set aside for himself the law which he had appointed for the human race, but sanctified every age [phase of human development]."[2] When we declare an unconditional yes to the conditions of our existence, we are joining Christ in his incarnational project, our spiritual evolution. Examples of these conditions are impermanence, change, injustice, suffering, betrayal, plans failing, people not coming through. An unconditional yes is a path to evolving into the image of Jesus who accepted all that happened in his human story. Our human story turns out to be the story of how our evolution into the risen Christ happens, how individual consciousness becomes cosmic.

There are also givens or traits that do not seem to change in our personality. There are choices we have made, now givens from the unalterable past. We carry regrets about some of them. There are also present circumstances fraught with anxiety that make us believe we are falling apart. They frighten us at times, but they highlight our connection with the human Jesus. In that sense of oneness with him, we come to trust that all our story fits into his accepting love. This is how Teilhard can say, "For those who love God everything can be transformed into good." With all its vagaries and disappointing betrayals, our human heart matters to Jesus. It is worth his incarnation and is worthy of joining him in resurrection.

Later, in the same section of *The Divine Milieu*, Teilhard uses the phrase "transfiguration of our diminishments" (DM, 49). Some things bring us down, make us feel less than we actually are or less than others, and ransack our confidence. These are the "diminishments" that await "transfiguration"—a word reminiscent of resurrection. How can spiritual consciousness help us in this area that is usually reserved for therapy?

It all happens in the same yes, the surrender to what is and what is emerging. St. Paul shows us who our model is when, speaking of Jesus, he says, "But in him it is always 'Yes'" (2 Cor 1:19). For most of us, as we have noted, this is our greatest challenge in the spiritual life, a surrender to what is, to who we are, to what has happened, is happening, and will happen to us. We so often fail to see that every happening shows us how to live Christ's cosmic and risen life on earth.

"Yes" is the only password we need as we face the struggles on our journey through life. It is another way of saying, "Thy will be done" because it is a yes to what we cannot change, only bow to. "Thy kingdom come" is our yes to the evolutionary emergence of God's limitless love.

Nothing is simply an event to grasp onto or run from, the sources of our suffering. Instead, we begin to look into what happens for a sacred opening to love more, know more, and be more. For instance, if someone betrays us, we say "Ouch!" grieve, and find an opportunity to love by being compassionate toward our hurt hearts with a firm resolve not to retaliate. At the same time, we feel compassion for others who suffer as we do *and* for those who cause suffering. This is how Christ's love comes alive in our personal story. This is how we live life more deeply and stay connected with everything and everyone. The cosmic Christ proclaims our cosmic calling. Now the Everything can reach the world through us.

For in him every one of God's promises is a "Yes."

—2 Corinthians 1:20

Prayer

I say Yes to everything that happens to me today as an
opportunity to give and receive love without reserve.
I am thankful for the enduring capacity to love that has
come to me from the Sacred Heart of the universe.
May everything that happens to me today open my heart
more and more.
May all that I think, say, feel, do, and am express loving-
kindness toward myself, those close to me, and all beings.

May love be my life purpose, my bliss, my destiny, my
calling—the richest grace I can receive or give.
And may I always be especially compassionate toward
people who are considered least or last or who feel
alone or lost.

FOR FURTHER REFLECTION

In the beginning was Power, intelligent, loving, energizing. In the beginning was the Word, supremely capable of mastering and molding whatever might come into being in the world of matter. In the beginning there were not coldness and darkness: there was Fire. (HU, 14)

If concern for progress and the cult of the earth are given as their final end the fulfillment of Christ, why should they not be transformed into a great virtue, as yet unnamed, which would be the widest form of the love of God, found and served in creation. (WTW, 65)

Lord Jesus, you who are gentle as the human heart, as fiery as the forces of nature, as intimate as life itself, in you I can melt away and with you I must have mastery and freedom. I love you as a world, as this world which has captivated my heart. It is you, I now realize, that my fellow humans, even those who do not believe, sense and seek throughout the magic immensities of the cosmos. (HU, 74)

Christ, through his Incarnation, is interior to the world, rooted in the world even in the heart of the tiniest atom. (SC, 36)

Like lightning, like a conflagration, like a flood, the attraction exerted by the Son of Man will lay hold of all the whirling elements in the universe so as to reunite them or subject them to his body. (DM, 130)

We must try everything for Christ; we must hope everything for Christ....That...is the true Christian attitude. To divinize does not mean to destroy, but to sur-create. We shall never know all that the Incarnation still expects of the world's potentialities. We shall never put enough hope in the growing unity of mankind. (DM, 134)

Glorious Lord Christ, the divine influence secretly diffused and active in the depths of matter, and the dazzling center where the innumerable fibers of the manifold meet: power as implacable as the world and as warm as life, you whose forehead is of the whiteness of snow, whose eyes are of fire, and whose feet are brighter than molten gold; you whose hands imprison the stars; you are the first and the last, the living and the dead and the risen again;... it is you to whom my being cried out with a desire as vast as the universe: "In truth you are my Lord and my God." (HU, 28)

6

THE SACRED HEART
OF THE UNIVERSE

*Divine fire…consume me and I will not resist….Your
lively flames make those live who die in them….Sacred
Heart of Jesus…inflame my heart with the divine love
with which your own is all on fire.*

—Letters of Margaret Mary Alacoque

Alice MacDonald has noted that "for St. Margaret Mary, fire, which is typically associated with hell, became the fire of divine love. For Teilhard, the Sacred Heart became a divine pledge that the universe of matter will not end by fire but be reborn in it. For him, at the heart of Matter was a lovingly beating world-heart, the burning heart of God. It was a heart on fire. God was manifesting divine love from and within the heart of Matter."[1]

Teilhard's spirituality revolved around his childhood and adult devotedness to the Sacred Heart of Jesus. He tells us, "It would be difficult for me to convey, how deeply and forcefully my life developed under the sign of the Heart of Jesus" (HM, 43). Teilhard gives us an example of how his devotion took shape in cosmic terms. While serving as a stretcher bearer during World War I, he went into a church and sat meditating on a picture of the Sacred Heart. He was suddenly graced with a mystical vision:

> The moment I saw a mysterious patch of crimson and gold delineated in the very center of the Savior's Breast, I found what I was looking for....It was the immersion of the Divine in the Corporeal....There was no longer a patch of crimson in the center of Jesus, but a glowing core of fire, whose splendor embraced every contour—first those of the God-Man—and then those of all things that lay within his ambiance. (HM, 43, 44)

We learn from science that the center of the earth is molten. Teilhard spoke of fire as the Heart of God aflame with love for us, setting everything ablaze with a new life. For Teilhard, the Heart of Jesus is the "universal blaze," the heart and animator of the universe. We recall Jesus saying, "I came to bring fire to the earth, and how I wish it were already kindled!" (Luke 12:49).

I remember in Catholic high school learning that if I received communion on nine consecutive first Fridays, I was assured of not dying without receiving the last rites. How important that was to me! How lucky I felt! Years later, my appreciation of Teilhard's work opened me to a new importance, a reality so much bigger than the high school version of the promise. Now, I would say that my joy is in a faith based on a sense of connection with all people in and through the Sacred Heart of Jesus. Now, I am offering my nine Fridays so that all people can find consolation in their dying moments, so that all people can feel Jesus holding them now and at the hour of death, so that all people can live and die in the Heart—rather than a feared judgment—of God.

The Sacred Heart does not refer to a cardiac muscle. It is a symbol and affirmation that love is the inner core of our being, our point of contact with the divine. It is the spiritual place in us where we meet and are the oneness that is "more deep and wide than that we have for ourselves," as St. Augustine writes in his *Confessions*.[2]

The Sacred Heart is a symbol and source of limitless love. How can we love limitlessly? It happens by a gift of grace offered to all of us. We practice loving that way when we do what evolution does—continually advance in wisdom-consciousness and love-connectedness. We dedicate this advance to our fellow humans, especially those who have not yet responded to this good news. Our mission is to find ways to evolve together toward more and more consciousness and connectedness. A mature devotion to the Sacred Heart takes us into this cosmic experience of our faith.

The Sacred Heart of Jesus is the Heart of the mystical body of the universe that was born from divine love. We are here to continue the universe's love story, the one that originated at the beginning of time. The "Constitutions of the Society of the Sacred Heart" state, "In all circumstances of life, wherever our mission leads us, our sole purpose in living is to glorify the Heart of Jesus, to discover and make known his love." Associates of the Sacred Heart speak of seeing the world from the open Heart of Jesus. This means both contemplation and apostolic awareness of the needs and sufferings of humanity and the planet. With eyes of caring love we are called to ponder what happens to our fellow humans and our world. We then take action to be of service and to share the good news about how open the Heart of Jesus is to everyone. In mystical devotion, our life purpose is thus the same as that of the Sacred Heart itself: to feel and demonstrate intense love for humanity and the planet on which we live—"God *so* loved the world" (John 3:16, emphasis added).

The realization that the world has a living heart is not limited to Christian theology. Here are two voices from very different traditions that were touched by the same awareness:

> At Epidauros, in the stillness, in the great peace that came over me, I heard the heart of the world beat. I know what the cure is: it is to give up, to relinquish, to

surrender, so that our little hearts may beat in unison with the great heart of the world.[3]

At the center of the Universe is a loving heart that continues to beat and that wants the best for every person. Anything that we can do to help foster the intellect and spirit and emotional growth of our fellow human beings, that is our job. Those of us who have this particular vision must continue against all odds. Life is for service.[4]

MEDITATION

Your main purpose in this revealing to us of your Heart was to enable our love to escape from the constrictions of the too narrow, too precise, too limited image of you which we had fashioned for ourselves. What I discern in your breast is simply a furnace of fire; and the more I fix my gaze on its ardency the more it seems to me that all around it the contours of your body melt away and become enlarged beyond all measure, till the only features I can distinguish in you are those of the face of a world which has burst into flame. (HU, 28)

Reflection

The revelations of the Sacred Heart of Jesus to mystics throughout the ages and to St. Margaret Mary in the seventeenth century have a powerful and thrilling message: Jesus offers to exchange his Heart with ours. People have always been seeking God, but in the revelations of the Sacred Heart, we learn that God seeks us, love has come looking for us, to give us the Heart that loves without limit. God receives our heart in exchange to show divine utter acceptance of us. We might add here that in a cosmic view, we can also go beyond exchange to *merger*—our hearts are one in the Heart of Christ.

We seek God because we long for transcendence, something beyond what we see, someone who loves us unconditionally and everlastingly. St. John shows us the reason we love God: "We love because he first loved us" (1 John 4:19). Love makes love possible. God has been seeking and loving us long before we sought or loved God. William of Saint-Thierry comments, "You first loved us so that we might love you. And that was not because you needed to be loved by us, but because we could not be what you created us to be, except by loving you."[5] We are made for love by Love. We are only fully ourselves when we love. This is because God who is love lives in our hearts. Without love and loving we are heartless.

We cannot become what God meant us to be, live up to our real identity, except by expanding our capacity to love until it includes all beings. We cannot become what we truly are psychologically, except by showing our unique brand of love. In both areas, spiritual and psychological, Jesus is our model:

- He extended his love without limit to all beings, saints and sinners alike.
- He loved the people in his world with a uniquely caring compassion and personal attentiveness.

These qualities describe our own calling to open our capacity to love by recklessly giving and unstintingly including.

Our devotion to the Sacred Heart is not about holding Jesus to promises made to us. It is about holding his Heart in the world with our own promise never to abandon it. We promise to love all that is. A holy project in the Church today can then be to upgrade devotion to the Sacred Heart in accord with this cosmic love consciousness. Such devotion does not have to be limited to standard prayers or practices. Moved by Teilhard's mystical consciousness, we can respond personally: Teilhard felt that the cosmos was developing a personality, that of the risen Christ. This is like saying the cosmos has a heart. The object of my devotion is therefore not an object separate from me, the standard image of the Sacred Heart, but an image of the entire cosmos, the reality of me, everyone, all things, the reality of God-in-matter. That is what penetrates and draws me to devotion to the Sacred Heart.

In Teilhard's vision outlined at the opening of this reflection, the familiar face and body of Jesus fade, and all he sees is the Sacred Heart ablaze in the center of the galaxies. Teilhard's vision of the Sacred Heart as the center of the universe has moved and opened my own faith to accommodate the same enlarged vision. Teilhard, my wise catechist, helps this happen by his visions and words. For as St. Madeleine Sophie Barat, foundress of the Society of the Sacred Heart, states, "Within the Sacred Heart, you have no country but the whole universe."

The following responses are arising within me:

> To say that the Sacred Heart is the heart of the cosmos is to say that love is the force that moves and rules the world— no matter how dark and violent our times. A divine force of affection and gentleness is animating me here and now, always and everywhere.
>
> To say that the heart of the world is the Heart of God is to say it is ever alive—no matter how death-dealing our times. Now I feel my own aliveness as one with the life force of the planet. Who God is, who I am, what all things are is one heart life force. This force wants to show itself in all I am and in how I live.

Here is the creed that my cosmic faith now leads me to affirm:

> I trust that I and all things were made in the image of Christ, the universal human, divine consciousness incarnate, humanity's eternal friend. I trust that I am here to live

in the likeness of Christ. I trust that the direction of evolution is toward his achieving in this world and time his full stature of love, wisdom, and healing of divisions. I am here to help that happen. Then I can have the same heart in me that is in Christ: planetary in concern and universal in love.

The Sacred Heart is the heart of the universe and of me. In such a mystical cosmic consciousness, I feel my way of praying changing. I no longer pray only for what I want for myself but always also for the welfare of all beings. I am here for the same reason the Sacred Heart of Jesus is here, to show and be the limitless love that is God.

My devotion to the Sacred Heart cannot be limited to whether I will find a way to get to heaven. It is out for higher stakes: cocreating with Jesus a kingdom that will make this earth the heaven it was meant to be. All is heaven when a heart is its center. All is heart when I and all of us have in ourselves the same immense intense "so" that God had when "God *so* loved the world." To look into the hearts of Jesus and Mary is to behold the disenfranchised, victimized, tortured, rejected people of the world held in an embrace of divine compassion. The hearts of Jesus and Mary wait for our human compassion to activate so the kingdom of justice can come to pass.

This is my morning offering:

Jesus, may all that happens to me today
open my heart to Your limitless love.
May all that happens lead me to love limitlessly.
Thank you for the graces You beam without ceasing
on me and all the cosmos.
I dedicate everything that I think, say, feel, do, and am
to cocreating with You a world of justice, peace, and love.

May the Hearts of Jesus and Mary be with me here,
now, and always.

Prayer: Cosmic Litany of the Sacred Heart

*Heart of Jesus, worthy of unending honor, alive in me to
love the world.*

*Heart of Jesus, from the heart of Mary, alive in me to love
the world.*

*Heart of Jesus, center of my heart, alive in me to love the
world.*

*Heart of Jesus, desire of the everlasting hills, alive in me to
love the world.*

*Heart of Jesus, center and joy of nature, alive in me to love
the world.*

*Heart of Jesus, life force of the universe, alive in me to love
the world.*

*Heart of Jesus, gate of Paradise, alive in me to love the
world.*

*Heart of Jesus, aglow with divine love, alive in me to love
the world.*

*Heart of Jesus, loving intent behind every twist of fate,
alive in me to love the world.*

*Heart of Jesus, pierced to open, never to close, alive in me
to love the world.*

*Heart of Jesus, treasury of mystical wisdom, alive in me to
love the world.*

*Heart of Jesus, from whose fullness we all receive, alive in
me to love the world.*

*Heart of Jesus, bountiful to all who turn to you, alive in
me to love the world.*

*Heart of Jesus, fountain of grace and holiness, alive in me
to love the world.*

Heart of Jesus, source of all consolation, alive in me to love the world.

Heart of Jesus, pledge of eternal loving-kindness, alive in me to love the world.

Heart of Jesus, mercy upon mercy, alive in me to love the world.

Heart of Jesus, source of all compassion, alive in me to love the world.

Heart of Jesus, freedom from fear, alive in me to love the world.

Heart of Jesus, full of generosity and healing, alive in me to love the world.

Heart of Jesus, my life, my death, my resurrection, alive in me to love the world.

Heart of Jesus, unfailing grace to those who live in you, alive in me to love the world.

Heart of Jesus, unending hope to those who die in you, alive in me to love the world.

Heart of Jesus, in whom there is only Yes, alive in me to love the world.

Jesus, I now think of myself as living solely for your Sacred Heart.

—Pope John XXIII

FOR FURTHER REFLECTION

The Heart of Christ at the heart of matter...the Golden Glow... gleaming at the heart of matter. (Letter to Jeanne-Marie Martier)

I also now realize the sacred heart is not a picture. There is a picture of it but the heart itself is the center and circumference of all the universe....Our Lord's Heart is indeed ineffably beautiful and satisfying: it exhausts all reality and answers all the soul's needs. The very thought of it is almost more than the mind can compass. (Letter to his cousin Marguerite)

I was still not yet "in theology" when, through and under the symbol of the "Sacred Heart," the Divine had already taken on for me the form, the consistence and the properties of an energy, of a fire: by that I mean that it had become able to insinuate itself everywhere, to be metamorphosed into no matter what. (HM, 44)

Throughout my life, through my life, the world has, little by little, caught fire in my sight until, aflame all around me, it has become almost completely luminous from within....Such has been my experience in contact with the earth, the diaphany of the divine at the heart of the universe on fire....Christ, his heart a fire: capable of penetrating everywhere, and gradually, spreading everywhere.... Our spiritual being is continually nourished by the countless energies of the tangible world....No power in the world can prevent us from savoring its joys because it happens at a level deeper than any power; and no power in the world, for the same reason, can compel it to appear. (DM, 9)

I adhere to the creative power of God; I coincide with it; I become not only its instrument but its living extension....This commerce... enables me to liken myself, ever more strictly and indefinitely, to God....I merge myself, in a sense, through my heart, with the very heart of God. (DM, 26)

The moment came when I could make out at the apex of the developing movement a marvellous conjunction, no longer a simple and vague conjunction between Christ and Matter—but rather a union between a Christ distinctly perceived as "the evolutioner" and a cosmic Source positively recognized as "Evolution"....The universalized Heart of Christ coincides with the heart of Matter transformed by love. (HM, 49)

EVERYTHING ABLAZE

Sacred Heart
Motor of evolution
Heart of Matter
World Zest
Heart of the World's Heart
Focus of ultimate and Universal energy
Center of the Cosmic Sphere of Cosmogenesis
Heart of Jesus, Heart of Evolution, unite me to
    yourself.

—Teilhard, "My Litany"[6]

3-24-18
From Teilhard's version of the
Sacred Heart... Its radiance
spread.
As the sun's rays pierce the
atmosphere —
So does the Sacred Son
                    Son

7

THE DIVINE FEMININE AND MARY

There is no word "impossible" for God. And this is precisely the task, to achieve what at first glance seems quite impossible: to unite Heaven and Earth, Flesh and Spirit, the World and God, Masculine and Feminine, Secular and Sacred.

—Raimon Panikkar, *Blessed Simplicity*

Every human has the energy of receptiveness as well as of active manifestation. The receptiveness energy is associated with the feminine archetype and the energy of actively manifesting is associated with the masculine archetype.[1] Both are required in any process of creation. Each evokes the other; each is activated by the other; each complements the other. In his hymn poem, "The Eternal Feminine," Teilhard depicts the archetypal feminine doing what love does—uninterruptedly unifying.

In her "Antiphon for Divine Wisdom," Hildegard of Bingen speaks of Sophia as the cosmic and eternal feminine principle in

God. Notice how her hymn shows an all-inclusive, all-connecting energy in the divine feminine:

> Sophia!
> you of the whirling wings,
> circling, encompassing
> energy of God:
>
> you quicken the world in your clasp.
>
> One wing soars in heaven,
> one wing sweeps the earth,
> and the third flies all around us.
>
> Praise to Sophia!
> Let all the earth praise her!

We see the creative power of Sophia also in Proverbs, where we read that Wisdom is "endowing with wealth those who love me, / and filling their treasuries. The LORD created me at the beginning of his work, / the first of his acts of long ago. / Ages ago I was set up, / at the first, before the beginning of the earth" (Prov 8:21–23). We notice here the similarity with the masculine counterpart: "All things came into being through him, and without him not one thing came into being" (John 1:3).

This divine feminine wisdom is honored as powerful: "She is a breath of the power of God, / and a pure emanation of the glory of the Almighty; / therefore nothing defiled gains entrance into her. / For she is a reflection of eternal light, / a spotless mirror of the working of God, / and an image of his goodness. / Although she is but one, she can do all things….For she is an initiate in the knowledge of God, / and an associate in his works" (Wis 7:25–27; 8:4).

Philo of Alexandria, a first-century Hellenic Jew, was a neo-Platonist who referred to the power and role of wisdom as the Logos, "the word," the principle that preexists, creates, and upholds the entire universe. The Gospel of John uses this masculine word to describe Christ, divine wisdom. Christ the Word, like Sophia, existed from all eternity with God. Logos and Sophia thereby signify two aspects of one and the same reality. Here is a striking example of identifying the coming of the Incarnate Word with Sophia: "Afterward she appeared on earth and lived with humankind" (Bar 3:37).

Our work in spiritually conscious evolution is to participate in Christ's evolutionary project: "I am making all things new" (Rev 21:5). We notice exactly the same affirmation referring to the divine feminine, Sophia: "She renews all things" (Wis 7:27). Our evolutionary work and appreciation of God in matter will continually enlist both masculine and feminine energies in all of us.

Sophia also refers to the way God manifests in our human story. Early mystics saw Sophia as caring for humanity: "She reaches mightily from one end of the earth to the other, / and she orders all things well" (Wis 8:1). We notice in this a similarity to a pagan prayer to Isis by Apuleius: "O Holy Blessed Lady....You are there when we call, stretching out your hand to push aside anything that might harm us. You even untangle the web of fate in which we may be caught, even stopping the stars for us if their pattern is in any way harmful."[2]

In special moments of mystical awareness among things in nature, we feel and know that what seems so separate is in fact one. We are touching into the wisdom of Sophia in the natural world. We are abiding in the real presence of God, with feminine and masculine energies, always within reach. Such mystical abiding can also happen in an event or with a person. Neither Sophia nor mystical awareness can be limited in how they appear to us, nor where they do so, when, in what or whom.

St. Paul also names Christ "the wisdom of God" (1 Cor 1:24). The famous church, Hagia Sophia, Holy Wisdom, was named for Christ by Constantine in the fourth century. Some Church fathers saw Sophia as the Holy Spirit, but most thought of Christ and Sophia as one, thus combining masculine and feminine energies— another affirmation of the mystical vision that has always been part of our faith Tradition.

Thomas Merton, in his prose poem "Hagia Sophia," expands on our theme with majestic clarity:

> There is in all visible things an invisible fecundity, a dimmed light, a meek namelessness, a hidden whole- ness. This mysterious Unity and Integrity is Wisdom, the Mother of all....There is in all things an inexhaust- ible sweetness and purity, a silence that is a fount of action and joy. It rises up in wordless gentleness and flows out to me from the unseen roots of all created being, welcoming me tenderly, saluting me with inde- scribable humility. This is at once my own being, my own nature, and the Gift of my Creator's Thought and Art within me, speaking as Hagia Sophia, speaking as my sister, Wisdom.[3]

Finally, we recall Genesis: "This is none other than the house of God, and this is the gate of heaven" (28:17). These two meta- phors for the natural world became two titles in the Litany of the Sacred Heart. They also appear as titles of Mary in the Litany of Loreto. Thus, the titles apply to masculine and feminine energies alike. Both titles likewise describe what earth is—a container of the divine, not separate from heaven but its open gate.[4]

> Your gates shall always be open;
> day and night they shall not be shut.

(Isa 60:11)

MEDITATION

Is it not the absolutely fertile generatrix, the Terra Mater, that carries within her the seeds of all life and the sustenance of all joy? Is it not at once the common origin of beings and the only end we could dream of, the primordial and indestructible essence from which all emerges and into which all returns, the starting point of all growth and the limit of all disintegration? (WTW, 30)

Reflection

In mystical intuition, the divine feminine is part of the wholeness of God. She is present at the beginning and evolves throughout the centuries as Mother Earth and Mother of All the Living, a title of Mary. She is passionately at work on our planet as Queen of Peace. She is always prompt in helping us grow to the stature of her Son. The divine feminine is the spiritual beauty of our beautiful world. The image of Mary represents what our planet and all of us look like in the eyes of God.

In our personal spirituality, we feel comfort in seeing Mary's relationship to us in three New Testament scenes:

Mary held the infant Jesus and she holds us in a dangerous world.
Mary held Jesus at the foot of the cross, and she is holding us in our sufferings.
Mary sat with the apostles at Pentecost as she is sitting beside us when the Holy Spirit comes upon us in Pentecostal fire, now and anytime.

In our personal devotion, we feel so strongly that Mary can be trusted to give all three of these comforts to us because she loves us both as individuals and as a collective humanity. The divine feminine indeed never has nor ever shall give up on us. To find her is to find the threshold into the spiritual world. She leads us to it and is the magnetic force beyond it to draw us into a mystical convergence with God's entire cosmos. She does all this because she is the mystery of wholeness beyond the fragments and rifts we see. When we look at her, we see the whole universe looking back at us with a welcoming, healing, and unifying smile.

Our model of the divine feminine, Mary, is not a spirit floating in the sky. One implication of her assumption into heaven, body and soul, is that she stays with us on our earthly journey. A sense of this companionship happens in a devout relationship to Mary. It can also happen when we feel the divine feminine energies and powers of Mary in one another. These are characterized in Mary, like the ancient goddesses, as virgin, mother, and wise queen. How can these energies awaken in us?

- We become focused on the divine in all things. This is the equivalent of virginal power, a one-pointedness, a directedness toward and openness to the cosmic Christ.
- We show nurturant love and caring connection to our planet. This is mother energy.
- We seek wisdom and use our powers wisely. This is wise woman and queen energy.

The divine feminine, in all three qualities, is continually moving through our world and lives. She is the fertile earth, the source of our liveliness, the cause of our joy. She is the diamond essence of the true self in us, the God-life beyond ego. She is the pearl of great price beyond greed. She is the light beyond ignorance.

When we turn to Mary, therefore, we are turning to earth. When we turn to Mary's heart, we are looking into the heart of the earth and into our own hearts. This is the mystical unity that we have longed for all our lives and have exuberantly found in Mary, human flesh, celestial soul. Teilhard, in *Toward the Future*, reminds us that "the spiritual power of matter lies in the spiritual power of the flesh and of the feminine" (TF, 70). Earth is the mother continually birthing and renewing us. Thus, prejudice against women is antipathy toward earth.

Do I trust the divine feminine in the world and in me? Do I believe the divine feminine works through me and in my commitment to the welfare of the world? Do I really believe that Mary is watching over our troubled world with grief and gifts? What makes me not call on her when I hear of so many disasters, acts of terror, war, torture, human slavery, ecological exploitation, human corruption, hate crimes? Don't I believe she can help with any and all of this? Have I come to think that only the force of law and arms can successfully deal with world conflicts and injustices? They have certainly not worked so far.

It is time for me to turn to Mary daily, to consign every news item to her loving and powerful heart. I want to hear the news of what is happening as a cosmic Christian, not only as a resident citizen. I want to be of service to the world by placing it in the hands of the trusted divine feminine, hands that have held it nurturantly from the Big Bang until the most recent suicide bombing. Then I become what I am called to be, what Mary was called to be, the container and deliverer of Jesus to a wanting, waiting, wavering world.

Prayer to the Divine Feminine

Bursting Virgin, expect me
Mother most brooding, hatch me in time
Nurse of the Milky Way, press me to you
Madonna of earth and sky, hold me with both hands
Mistress of hearths, my shelter be
Escort of journeys, accompany me
Woman of mystery, make sense of me

EVERYTHING ABLAZE

Lady of light, see through me, see me through
Dame of the dark, clutch me in the abyss
Grandmother of sorrows, grieve with me
Queen of swords, slash and save me
Rose of thorns, bud me to bloom
Maiden of meaning, deeply involve me
Bride of the Spirit, wholly dissolve me
Full of grace you and I and all that is
Now and at the hour of awakening.

FOR FURTHER REFLECTION

When the world was born, I came into being. God instilled me into
the initial multiple as a force of condensation and concentration.
In me is seen that side of beings by which they are joined as one,
in me the fragrance that makes them hasten together and leads
them, freely and passionately, along their road to unity. Through
me, all things have their movement and are made to work as one.
I am the beauty running through the world, to make it associate
in ordered groups: the ideal held up before the world to make it
ascend. (WTW, 192)

I am the essential Feminine....In the stirring of the layers of the cosmic substance, whose nascent folds contain the promise of worlds
beyond number, the first traces of my countenance could be read....
See my image playing over the surface of the divine fire. And at that
moment you may see with wonder how there unfolds, in the long
web of my charms, the ever-living series of allurements—of forces
that one after another have made themselves felt ever since the bor-
derline of nothingness, and so brought together and assembled the
elements of Spirit—through love. (WTW, 192, 201–2)

For the man who has found me, the door to all things stands open.
I extend my being into the soul of the world—not only through
the medium of that man's own sensibility, but also through the
physical links of my own nature—or rather, I am the magnetic

72

force of the universal presence and the ceaseless ripple of its smile. I open the door to the whole heart of creation: I, the Gateway of the Earth, the Initiation. He who takes me, gives himself to me, and is himself taken by the universe. (WTW, 194–95)

Woman is, for man, the symbol and personification of all the fulfillment we look for from the universe. (TF, 70)

The world's energies and substances…produced the glittering gem of matter, the Pearl of the Cosmos, and the link with the incarnate personal Absolute—the Blessed Virgin Mary, Queen and Mother of all things, the true Demeter [Divine Mother]. (WTW, 59)

Seeing the mystic immobile, crucified or rapt in prayer, some may perhaps think that his activity is in abeyance or has left this earth: they are mistaken. Nothing in the world is more intensely alive and active than purity and prayer, which hang like an unmoving light between the universe and God. Through their serene transparency flow the waves of creative power charged with natural virtue and with grace. What else but this is the Virgin Mary? (WTW, 144)

When God decided to realize His Incarnation before our eyes, He had first of all to raise up in the world a virtue capable of drawing Him as far as ourselves. He needed a mother who would engender Him in the human sphere. What did he do? He created the Virgin Mary, that is to say He called forth on earth a purity so great that, within this transparency, He would concentrate Himself to the point of becoming a little child. There, expressed in its strength and reality, is the power of purity to bring the divine to birth among us…."Blessed are you who have believed"….It is in faith that purity finds the fulfillment of its fertility. (DM, 109)

8

THE CHURCH AND RELIGION

No longer simply a religion of individuals and of heaven, but a religion of mankind and of the earth—that is what we are looking for at this moment.

—Pierre Teilhard de Chardin, *Activation of Energy*

This understanding of religion makes the Church a new creation, intended to be what Teilhard called a "phylum of love." It is not only an institution but the palpable presence of the Holy Spirit in the act of evolving our world. Teilhard sees evolution as a journey to God, not only individually but in community. We appreciate this in our corresponding belief in the Church as a Communion of Saints, a community that helps one another on both sides of the grave. The Church is thus meant to be the advancer and advocate of the human journey. It can only do this with a program that encompasses mystical consciousness as well as evolutionary spirituality. An unchanging institutional style does not get us there.

Disappointed with how this was not happening in his day, Teilhard had serious issues with the bureaucratic system in the

Church: "It has sometimes seemed to me there are three weak stones sitting dangerously in the foundations of the modern Church: first, a government that excludes democracy; second, a priesthood that excludes and minimizes women; third, a revelation that excludes, for the future, prophecy" (Letter to Christophe de Gaudefroy, 1929).

Teilhard also suffered personal difficulties with the official Church regarding his teachings and ideas. Rather than engage in an ongoing dialogue with him, the Church silenced his important and challenging voice.

Yet in the midst of all this, Teilhard remained faithful to the Church. Years later, in 1951, in a letter to Father General Jean-Baptiste Janssens, SJ, he wrote, "I now feel more indissolubly bound to the hierarchical Church and to the Christ of the Gospel than ever before in my life. Never has Christ seemed to me more real, more personal or more immense." That word "immense" shows that Teilhard never lost sight of the bigness of the Church, stretching far beyond the boundaries of the city of Rome. In cosmic consciousness, the Church of Christ includes all people of good will. The Church then encompasses all those on the human-divine journey to the Omega of *agape*, that is, selfless and universal love.

What is religion? All religions have four elements in common: a set of beliefs, a moral code, specific rituals, and various forms of devotion that foster a personal relationship to God. What do these four components of religion look like in a natural mysticism like Teilhard's?

Beliefs become pathways into mystery. They are not dogmatic certainties but thrive on ever-evolving intuitions. They ultimately elude the logical mind. In a mystical orientation, we let go of speculating about beliefs and live by experiential faith.

A *moral code* explicates and distinguishes right from wrong. An example is the Ten Commandments, which outline the minimum requirements of a morally upright life. A mystical morality

75

includes ethical precepts, but focuses intensely on an unconditionally caring connection between us and all beings. In Teilhard's
view, this includes planetary awareness, what today we understand as an enduring commitment to the environment.

Rituals happen in nature, not only in church. They can be
spontaneous rather than tied to a specific formula. They enact
mystical consciousness and thus make every table an altar, every
transformation a transfiguration. Rituals are rites of passage in
the journey from duality to a sense of our—and the universe's—
unalterable union with God.

Devotion includes, but is ultimately about more than, a personal relationship to God. It is passion and zeal for all beings and
for the cosmos too. This planetary mystical consciousness makes
every day an evolutionary opportunity. We see ourselves not as
observers of evolution but as votaries, devotees of the divinely
begun and divinely led process of development that is happening
here and everywhere, always and already, now and eternally.

Teilhard hoped that the Church would become the container
and proclaimer of these enlightened realizations. We can then
emphasize not the differences between religions, but rather an all-
inclusive religious consciousness. The Church would not be paro-
chial, but cosmic in every parish. We see this happening more and
more nowadays. As a community of faith, the Church continually
responds to the Master's call to love and serve all humanity and
earth. This is how she arouses us to share joyously the message—
and Heart—of Jesus. We are Church in any moment when we are
Jesus in the world. Then we draw our brothers and sisters to the
gospel because they are touched by how much it means to us and
how loving it makes us toward them.

When we act lovingly toward others, we are also making
direct contact with Jesus who said, "'Truly I tell you, just as you
did it to one of the least of these who are members of my family,
you did it to me'" (Matt 25:40). Jesus never gives a command

without including an invitation to us to draw nearer to his Heart, to be his Heart.

Finally, the Church is devoted to truth both as stable and as evolving, formed both in a historic faith community and by individual experience. Pope Francis, in an open letter in September 2015 to journalist and atheist Eugenio Scalfari, wrote,

> I would not speak about "absolute" truths, even for believers....Truth is a relationship. As such, each one of us receives the truth and expresses it from within, that is to say, according to one's own circumstances, culture, and situation in life....So we grow in the understanding of the truth....There are ecclesiastical rules and precepts that were once effective, but now they have lost value or meaning. The view of the Church's teaching as a monolith to defend without nuance or different understandings is wrong.[1]

The Pope's musings reflect the mystical style of honoring our inner experience of the many and innovative shapes truth may take. This fellow Jesuit of Teilhard seems intent on carrying his lively message to the Church today.

MEDITATION

> Since my childhood...I have always loved and sought to read the face of nature; but even so, I can say that my approach has not been that of the scientist but that of the votary. It seems to me that every effort I have made, even when directed to a purely natural object, has always been a religious effort, substantially, it has been one single effort. (HM, 198)

Reflection

Our awe in nature began in childhood when we asked questions about the blueness of the sky or the shape of lightning. The sense of wonder about natural things is a religious experience since the cosmos is God's body in visible form. The sacraments demonstrate this, for each of them brings us to God through natural things.

Elaine Pagels, in *The Gnostic Gospels*, wrote, "The orthodox Christian saw Christ not as one who leads souls out of this world into enlightenment, but as 'fullness of God' come down into human experience—into *bodily* experience—to sacralize it."[2] The Church on earth is a spiritual collective composed of bodily beings in a world of matter. We are the Church and we exist in this natural world. The Church's calling therefore is to be deeply involved in what the world needs from us, what sustains it best, and what our place in it can be. The purpose of the Church is to increase consciousness and connection, the same purposes we see in evolution. When we act with loving compassion toward all beings, we as Church acknowledge Christ as the pivot of all convergence, all consciousness, all connection.

In mature religious awareness, the Church is a happening, a verb, not a noun. It happens when two or three are gathered to cocreate the kingdom of God. It happens when anyone honors the natural world and does what he or she can to preserve it. The connection between the Church and nature was not usually talked about in our religious upbringing. In *Laudato Si'*, Pope Francis has highlighted as crucial in his revisioning of religion the affection for and shepherding of our planet.

Teilhard did not limit faith to being simply an assent to a belief system. He paid rapt attention to the way faith was continually evolving in his own soul. He noticed that the development of his faith paralleled the progress of his scientific knowledge of the universe. We can do the same. In a mystical spirituality, we come to appreciate the oneness of knowledge. Then there is not a scientific truth alongside a religious truth. All truth is one and from the Holy Spirit as St. Thomas Aquinas noted long ago. We have heard of "the death of God" in our modern world, a giving up of the search for God. But we can trust that we are still seeking God alive in every search for new knowledge about the cosmos. Educating ourselves about the environment in order to preserve it is therefore a religious act.

Our contemporary rituals await an enlarging "proportional to the newly discovered immensities of a universe whose aspect exceeds the present compass of our power of worship" (FM, 268). This is our challenge in Church teaching and worship today. We do see some signs of enlarging our experience of worship. For instance, in our prayers and social projects, there is more focus on world events and more concern about the planet. Such global consciousness is now recognized as deeply spiritual. There is a collective transformation afoot in the world at large, a planetary awareness. We join it by expanding our sense of Church and religion so that they can accommodate the bigness we now see and even more exultantly foresee.

Global consciousness becomes spiritual practice when we engage in global action. Perhaps our sense of awe in nature happens so that we can respond to her in a caretaking way. Nature woos us to become her beloved. This will lead us to respond to her needs with alacrity. We then commit ourselves to take a stand to save our too threatened resources. Our sense of wonder in nature joined with our commitment to the preservation of the earth includes all that religion and the Church include: faith, integrity, ritual, and devotion.

Nothing less is required of us as Church than what Teilhard refers to as an enduring belief in the world as the right place for the ever-unfolding incarnation. This realization also gives us a sense of the sacred in matter, what religion is meant to cherish and protect. In our felt faith, we are fully trusting that all of nature, the cosmos in its entirety, is a tabernacle. It is always and already holding the holy of holies and the bread of life. We find the sacred, the holy of holies, by a peek into the cosmos. We find spiritual nurturance there too since every earth grain is holy and eucharistic in the tabernacle of God's earth. This is the good news we delightedly awaken to in the natural mysticism of Teilhard.

As Pope Francis has reminded us, caring for the earth is the essence of religious devotion and of the Church's calling. Then, indeed, the natural world is our holy Church and the cosmos is the Body of Christ. Our world is not only a place on a map; it is a treasure chest of the divine. Our Church is not only our religious affiliation; it is a mission to earth.

A mystical view that includes both the Church and religion opens us to an abiding sense of God's presence in the world, in us, in all beings. This presence is not simply a sense of "someone there." It is a sense of Someone with us, Emmanuel—God with us. The presence is thus an *accompaniment*. We may not always feel the companionship palpably, but we do trust it. We can feel God staying with us in the presence of the Blessed Sacrament. In fact, the word *companion* refers to sharing bread. We know who does that with his own Body.

We can feel accompaniment in nature too: Standing under a tree can give us the feeling of being watched over by comforting arms. Standing under the stars can give us the feeling of being beheld by twinkling eyes. Standing in a cave can give us the feeling of being safely contained, bats our sentinels. Swimming can give us the sense of reliable buoyancy no matter how rough the waves. God is abiding accompaniment in all these very same senses—staying, watching over, beholding, containing, creating buoyancy in the spikey waters of life. The Church, too, is here to be the Good Shepherd accompanying our evolving selves in all those same senses. And as the Church in the world, we are the loyal companions of our fellow wonderers.

*When Moses says, "Who am I that I should go to
Pharaoh?" God answers not by telling Moses who he is,
but by telling him who God is, saying, "I will be with you"
(Exodus 3:12).*

—Harold Kushner, *Overcoming
Life's Disappointments*

Prayer (Based on Psalm 23)

*Jesus, with You as my shepherd
I never want for anything.
You gave me this beautiful planet
With green pastures and life-giving waters.
They refresh me, body, mind, heart, and soul.
Your Gospel shows me the right paths on my journey.
Now when I walk through a dark valley,
I'm not afraid anymore,
Because I know You are right here beside me,
My caring companion.
You keep showing me the ways You protect and guide me.
You made a place for me at Your messianic banquet.
You anointed me with an earth oil of gladness.
I am thankful for the abundance You share with me.
Surely love and goodness shall grace me all my life
And I will dwell in this wonderful world, the House of the
    Lord,
And be to the world a Shepherd like You.*

FOR FURTHER REFLECTION

The Church, the reflectively Christified portion of the world, the Church, the principal focus of inter-human affinities through super-charity, the Church, the central axis of universal convergence and the precise point of contact between the universe and Omega Point. (*My Fundamental Vison*, 191–92)

The only reason that can decide me to adhere to a religion must... consist in the harmony of a higher order which exists between that religion and the individual creed to which the natural evolution of my faith has led me. (CE, 120)

Even in spite of ourselves, every day [we are becoming] more one in our common thoughts and enthusiasms....[It seems] less possible...to dismiss the evidence that we are, here and now, the subjects of a profound organic transformation that is collective in type. (SC, 159)

The more dangerous a thing, the more is its conquest ordained by life: it is from that conviction that the modern world has emerged; and from that our religion, too, must be reborn. (TF, 75)

"To be ready" has never seemed to me to signify anything else than "to be stretching forward." What the world expects from the Church of God is a generalization and deepening of the meaning of the Cross....In a universe which is in the way of unification with God, the Cross (without losing its expiatory and compensatory function) becomes, even more surely, the symbol and expression of evolution as a whole....That is what I believe, and that is what I so long to confess publicly before I die. (Letter to Pere Andre Ravier, SJ)

In presenting the Christian doctrine of salvation, it must not be forgotten that the world, taken as a whole, that is to say in so far as it consists in a hierarchy of souls which appear only successively, develop only collectively, and will be completed only in union with the world...undergoes a sort of vast ontogenesis (a vast becoming what it is)....Beneath our efforts to put spiritual form into our own lives, the world slowly accumulates, starting with the whole of matter, that which will make of it the Heavenly Jerusalem or the New Earth. (DM, 24)

If, as the result of some interior revolution, I were to lose in succession my faith in Christ, my faith in a personal God, and my faith in spirit, I feel that I should continue to believe invincibly in the world. The world...is the first, the last, and the only thing in which I believe. It is by this faith that I live. (CE, 99)

9

✗ THE EUCHARIST

Grant, Lord, that your descent into the universal Species
may not be for me just something loved and cherished,
like the fruit of some philosophical speculation, but may
become for me truly a real Presence. Whether we like it
or not, by power and by right, you are incarnate in the
world, and we are all of us dependent upon you.

—Pierre Teilhard de Chardin, *Hymn of the Universe*

The host is a thing, a noun. The Eucharist is an action, a verb. We look at each of these forms of presence in the light of Teilhard's mystical vision: The Eucharistic host is Christ's body present to us sacramentally. The host remains matter chemically. In the mystical awareness of Teilhard, Spirit and matter become one.

- *Sacramentally*, the risen Christ is present in the host by the action of the Mass: "Jesus took a loaf of bread, and after blessing it he broke it, gave it to the disciples, and said, 'Take, eat; this is my body'" (Matt 26:26). This is a historical event that now gives us the same graces that came to the apostles at the Last Supper.

- *Mystically*, the risen Christ is present in all matter by the fact of creation: "All things came into being through him, and without him not one thing came into being" (John 1:3). This is a transhistorical happening that sees the cosmos in the Christ of universal consciousness and eternal presence.

Evolution is how Christ's mystical presence, in and as the cosmos, moves and animates us on our spiritual journey. Christ first said, "This is my Body," at the Big Bang, the bodying forth. At the Last Supper, Jesus was looking at the entire cosmos when he said, "This is my Body." Now we see how there is only one host and, in Teilhard's view, the universe is it. All matter is infused with Christ's life: "I firmly believe that everything around me is the body and blood of the Word" (HU, 21).

In the natural mysticism of Teilhard, the transubstantiation of matter at Mass reflects the transubstantiation of all matter into a divine presence. This is not only the presence of the risen Christ standing at the empty tomb. This is the Christ of the Andes whose arms embrace all peoples. Christ is then love and welcome to all beings. In that image, we find solace in the embrace of the cosmic Christ. We also accept the challenge to have arms like his so we can embrace all beings as bigheartedly as he does.

We know what is being offered to us in the Eucharist. We are finding the life given us in baptism, now being nourished. *We are being given our true nature, the spiritual reality of who we are in the depths of our being.* We hear Teilhard say it so directly: "In the Host, Lord Jesus, you offer me my life" (HU, 154). We also hear the same good news from St. Augustine: "If you want to understand the body of Christ, listen to the Apostle Paul speaking to the faithful: 'You are the body of Christ, member for member'" (1 Cor 12:27). If you, therefore, are Christ's body and members, it is your own mystery that is placed on the Lord's table! It is your own mystery that you are receiving! You are saying 'Amen' to what you are; your response is a personal signature, affirming your faith."[1]

The life we say "Amen" to is our own right now and that of the world around us. Stories and predicaments in the world accost us daily in the news. Personal struggles and sorrows beset us. At Mass, we can place them on the paten along with the bread. In mystical awareness, all this is Christ's body. Every joy and grief of our lives, and those of all of us, are Eucharist. What better news can there be than that?

In a deeply mystical sense, Mass is being celebrated now and always in our higher self. In the center of our being is enacted the supreme celebration of wholeness and transformation. Our spiritual practice in response is to mirror in our daily lives what the Holy Spirit is doing within us; we offer all that we are, we consecrate all that we do, we remain in communion—all for the welfare of our world.

We can appreciate the Eucharist as a limitless communion. We commune with Christ within; we are also communing with our faith community, the whole human community, and the natural world too. All beings are included in the ever-widening circle of our love shown in action, individual and social. It is this Christ of love ever reaching out through us that is consecrated and that is consecrating the world as well.

The Eucharist answers the question, "What is heaven like?" As we saw above, it is the Communion of Saints, the interchange of help and prayer among those in heaven, those suffering, those on the pilgrim way. Heaven is also the messianic banquet in which we find nourishment and fellowship in Christ. All our communions on this earth are foretastes of this banquet. Indeed, because of the Communion of Saints, all our communions are one communion. All our Masses are one Mass. All our Eucharists are one Eucharist. Every monstrance is exposing the precious value of matter. Every natural thing is a monstrance showing us a morsel of the Body of Christ. The Eucharist is the sacrament of limitless connectedness.

The Eucharist

*The rays from the image pierced the Sacred Host and
spread out all over the world.*

—St. Faustina, *Diary*, no. 441

MEDITATION

From the moment that you said "This is my Body," not
only the bread and wine on the altar, but to a certain
extent everything in the universe became yours and
nourishes in our souls the life of grace and the spirit….
The Holy Eucharist is in fact extended throughout the
universe and so constitutes a promise of its eventual
transfiguration….It captures all the power of loving in
the universe. (WTW, 146)

Reflection

In the presence of the Blessed Sacrament one day a few years
ago, I was graced with a sudden, life-changing vision. While looking at the host, I was aware of my belief that it is the body of
Christ. But in that moment, I suddenly saw the host as *matter*
and realized that I was adoring God in matter. I suddenly saw
all matter summed up in the material host. This reminded me of
Teilhard's mystical realizations that celebrate this same point. The
monstrance is the world holding the body of Christ in matter for
all to cherish and adore. In his essay, "The Monstrance," Teilhard
exclaimed in mystical wonder: "The whole world had become
incandescent, had itself become like a single giant Host."

Today, I connected this thought to the theme of Pope Francis's
encyclical *Laudato Si'*: "Everything is related, and we human beings
are united as brothers and sisters on a wonderful pilgrimage,
woven together by the love God has for each of his creatures and
which also unites us in fond affection with brother sun, sister

moon, brother river and mother earth" (no. 92). We enter mystical consciousness when all of nature is one host, when everything that is, is holy.

The challenge in our faith is to see in the exposition of the Blessed Sacrament not only a host to adore but a beatific vision to participate in here and now in our lifetime. We are looking at a display of our life mission, to be drawn to matter as a path to God and to draw all beings to God with us too. The rays of gold in the monstrance seem only to beam outward from Christ's body into the world. In mystical awareness, we see them also drawing all things into the host that is their center and destiny. The rays are both *tangential*, reaching out, and *radial*, drawing us in—to use two of Teilhard's words.

At Mass, the Eucharist is an experience of communion not only with those who are with us in church but with all beings everywhere. Teilhard speaks of this: "All the communions of all men, present, past, and future are one communion....There is only one Mass and one Communion....Right from the hands that knead the dough to those that consecrate it, the great and universal Host should be prepared in a spirit of adoration....The sacramental species is formed by the totality of the world and all the duration of the creation is needed for its consecration" (DM, 31, 96, 97).

The Eucharist at Mass is Christ present not only as our food for the journey. We are Christ as food for the world, a nurturant power for all. We are doing what he came to do, being what he is. The *Catechism of the Catholic Church* quotes St. Augustine: "Let us rejoice then and give thanks that we have become not only Christians, but Christ himself. Do you understand and grasp, brethren, God's grace toward us? Marvel and rejoice: *we have become Christ.*"[2]

We can celebrate our own personal Mass on the altar of the world. We can do what Teilhard did when he had no bread or wine. He offered all creation to God in a eucharistic way. We can do the same. Here is a practice that affirms a natural mysticism, a planetary consciousness: anywhere we feel an awe in nature, we

can spontaneously bring into our awareness three main parts of
the Mass, the offertory, the consecration, and the communion:

- *Offertory*: We offer all the natural world to God
  with a sense of praise and with thanksgiving for
  all it gives us. This is placing the things in nature
  on the paten of the offertory: "May what we offer
  become your body, Jesus."
- *Consecration*: We consecrate the natural world to
  be the body of the risen Christ always and already
  with us in any and every moment: "Father, send
  your Holy Spirit upon this moment (person/place/
  thing/event) so that it may become for us the living
  presence of your Son."
- *Communion*: We commune with nature and all
  humanity as resources of nurturance in Christ. We
  give ourselves to one another as spiritual nurturance,
  becoming to everyone what we believe Christ is to
  us: "May all we are and do become one communion
  through Christ, with Christ, and in Christ."

This practice brings the essentials of the Mass into what is special or important to us. We make the elements of the Mass a prayer
for ourselves and the world. We can do this at any time or in any
place—not only in nature. For instance, we can use this practice in
a busy city. We can also summon up this form of prayer in a crisis or
in any challenge. We can pray this way in response to any event or
relationship that is meaningful to us. In fact, nothing that happens
or that exists is beyond offering, consecrating, and communing.

In this prayer practice, we are becoming immediately aware of
the real presence of God in all that is and in all that happens. Our
practice is therefore a mystical, Mass-inspired prayer for all of us,
the priesthood of the faithful. We recall how we are described by
St. Peter: "You are a chosen people, a royal priesthood, a holy nation,

God's special possession, that you may declare the praises of him who called you out of darkness into his wonderful light" (1 Pet 2:9 NIV).

The eucharistic host is a sign and a reality. We do not simply adore the sign but open ourselves to becoming a eucharistic presence in the world. How can we do this? William Cavanaugh, in *Torture and the Eucharist*, wrote, "The Eucharist is the true 'politics,' as St. Augustine saw, because it is the public performance of the true eschatological or future City of God in the midst of another City which is passing away."[3] Yes, we make present here and now the kingdom of justice, peace, and love, the kingdom of the Eucharist. In that living Bread come down from heaven, we see Jesus the just, Jesus the peacemaker, Jesus the lover who has never ceased loving humanity with an everlasting love. The Eucharist takes effect in us when those three qualities become our own.

> *This view of the world, which I am here calling the Eucharistic Planet, a view of the world as the Real Presence of the Divine, of the Absolute, a view of the world as a single living Body, in which the various members freely give themselves as food to one another....A sense of the Eucharistic Planet, of the Real Presence of the Divine in the world, is something we need now for the protection of the planet.*

> —Beatrice Bruteau, "Eucharistic Ecology and Ecological Spirituality," *Cross Currents* 40, no. 4 (Winter 1990/91)

Prayer

We thank You God for showing us in the Eucharist who we really are: a unity of body and spirit, human and divine, without division, without exclusion of anyone or anything for all is sacred.

*When You look at us, You see us in the loving Heart of
Your Son who makes us all one, not only those of us at
the table at Mass but all humanity around the table of
the earth.*

*We partake of the body of the risen Christ, because we are
his Body and so is this whole cosmos.*

*Give us the grace to continue Your work of evolving the
Church and the world.*

*We thank You for creating the universe, and each of us,
through Christ the pioneer of our journey, and in the
Holy Spirit, the ever-enlivening gift of Your love*

FOR FURTHER REFLECTION

When Christ, extending the process of his incarnation, descends
into the bread in order to replace it, his action is not limited to
the material morsel which his presence will, for a brief moment,
volatilize: this transubstantiation is aureoled with a real though
attenuated divinizing of the entire universe. From the particular
cosmic element into which he has entered, the activity of the Word
goes forth to subdue and to draw into himself all the rest. (HU, 6)

I begin to understand: under the sacramental species it is primarily through the "accidents" of matter that you touch me, but, as a
consequence, it is also through the whole universe in proportion
as this ebbs and flows over me under your primary influence. In
a true sense, the arms and hands that you open to me are nothing less than all the united powers of the world which, penetrated
and permeated to their depths by your will, your tastes, and your
temperament, converge upon my being to form it, nourish it, and
bear it along toward the center of your fire. In the Host it is my life
that you are offering me, Jesus. (HU, 154)

To interpret adequately the fundamental position of the Eucharist
in the economy of the world....It is, I think, necessary that Christian thought and Christian prayer should give great importance to

the real and physical extensions of the Eucharistic Presence....As we properly use the term "our bodies" to signify the localized center of our spiritual radiations...so it must be said that in its initial and primary meaning the term "Body of Christ" is limited, in this context, to the consecrated species of Bread and Wine. The Host is comparable to a blazing fire whose flames spread out like rays all around it. ("My Universe")

Adherence to Christ in the Eucharist must inevitably, *ipso facto*, incorporate us a little more fully on each occasion in a Christogenesis which itself...is none other than the soul of universal cosmogenesis. ("Introduction to the Christian Life")

At the touch of the supersubstantial Word the immense host which is the universe is made flesh. Through your own incarnation, my God, all matter is henceforth incarnate. (HU, 17)

There appears to the dazzled eyes of the believer the Eucharistic mystery itself, extended infinitely into a veritable universal transubstantiation, in which the words of the Consecration are applied not only to the sacrificial bread and wine but, mark you, to the whole Mass of joys and sufferings produced by the Convergence of the World as it progresses. (HM, 94)

Over every living thing which is to spring up, to grow, to flower, to ripen during this day, say again the words: "This is my Body." Over every death force which is waiting to corrode, wither, or cut down, speak again your command: "This is my Blood." (HU, 15)

10

THE POWER OF ADORATION

To adore: that means to lose oneself in the unfathomable,
to plunge into the inexhaustible, to find peace in the
incorruptible, to be absorbed in defined immensity, to
offer oneself to the fire and the transparency, to annihilate
oneself in proportion as one becomes more deliberately
conscious to oneself, and to give of one's deepest to that
whose depth has no end.

—Pierre Teilhard de Chardin, *The Divine Milieu*

According to the dictionary, to adore is to worship and honor God. Adoration becomes dualistic when God is above us in the ether and we are earthbound here below.

In rituals, we use prayer, kneeling, chanting, and other external expressions of adoration. In mystical adoration, we may engage in these same activities, but we use them as stepping stones into silence and contemplation. In mystical adoration, we feel an intimacy with God so the sense of distance vanishes. Consequently, adoration becomes an entry into a mystery. We are no longer praying to a distant God. Our life is a prayer because the Holy Spirit prays *in* us. The poet, Christopher Smart, in "A Song to David," describes the prayer without dualism:

> Where ask is have, where seek is find,
>> Where knock is open wide.

Teilhard wrote, "There is much less difference than people think between research and adoration."[1] His sense of adoration was not about worshipping what is outside us. It was more a search for the truth about the universe. In his scientific research projects, Teilhard felt the same sense of adoration as in prayer. He was also swept up in work and prayer by a sense of awe, what he referred to as a dark adoration because its object remains ever hidden, ungraspable and ineffable. We recall this passage in Exodus, so descriptive of mystical experience: "The people stood at a distance, while Moses drew near to the thick darkness where God was" (Exod 20:21).

Based on Teilhard's view, adoration is an *attitude and a practice* with these elements:

- We surrender to a mystery; we give up having to know or having to be certain. Mystery does not refer to a meaning we don't understand. It is what is too full of and deep with meaning for minds as limited as ours to grasp.
- We focus not on what is graspable but surrender to what is too immense to hold on to. We go beyond definitions and accept that we exist in a cloud of unknowing. We likewise know there is nothing left to know.
- We give up our usually reliable—and limited— perspective in favor of what has no horizon. We give up finding a final version of truth.

- We give up our illusion of solid ground and are willing to admit we are on ever-moving ground. We no longer rely on our ego's version of safety and security. We have given up on ego as a refuge from anxiety or as an oracle offering solutions to all our perplexities.
- We find our serenity instead in what is spiritual. We no longer look only to intellectual or psychological techniques to find peace of mind. Our larger refuge is in a higher power that we contact by prayer and meditation.
- We offer ourselves totally to what might consume us. We are turning our wills over to the will of God, asking only for a knowledge of that will and the courage to carry it out.
- We become transparent, no hideouts, no escape hatches. Now we want to be seen just as we are. *We are not trying to look good only to be divine goodness in the world.*
- We go beyond our limited ego identity to a recognition of a higher consciousness in us, the divine within. We have found an identity beyond the one described on our driver's license. We now want to go by our name as it is spelled in heaven. We are no longer separate but linked to all beings.
- We give ourselves without reserve to what has no end and with no end in sight. We hold nothing back but surrender all that we have been, are, and will be to the eternal One of Oneness.

In all these ways, adoration mirrors exactly what is required for mystical consciousness. The eight points, based on the opening quotation by Teilhard, show us what adoration entails. They likewise describe what is meant by trust in God. Following them in daily life can help us move toward a mystical spirituality. They are also graces, accessible to any of us.

The fact that all the qualities of adoration are mystical, spiritual, practice oriented, and graced, shows clearly that adoring is about more than bending our knees. It is a new, egoless, courageous *lifestyle*. Adoration can become our entire manner, what we look like when we have grown up spiritually. Adoration is an attitude of real presence in a world that is always showing us a Real Presence. The sacred world of nature then, like the sacred host, becomes true tidings of comfort and joy.

Finally, we can look at one other meaningful implication in our nondual sense of adoration: What we adore, for instance, the Blessed Sacrament, is not simply an object. Our adoration does not go only in one direction, from us to it. There is an exchange, as in all sacraments. We receive what we worship; we become what we adore. In our adoration, each of us becomes a unique incarnation of the Body of Christ. This is how we are food for others, the living bread humanity is asking us for.

All places that the eye of heaven visits
Are to a wise man ports and happy havens.

—Shakespeare, *Richard II* (Act I, Scene 3)

MEDITATION

Receive, O Lord, this all-embracing host which your whole creation, moved by your magnetism, offers you at this dawn of a new day. (HU, 13)

Reflection

We are not only on the earth but of it. We do not own the earth; we are one with it. Adoration is acknowledging that connection. Then we pray *with* the earth. This happens once we see that all nature is a divine milieu, the home of God, the place God loves, a diaphany of God as love, the body of Christ, a tabernacle of the Holy Spirit.

This earth is still being created by the Father, divine creative energy, still extending the incarnation of the Son, divine redemptive energy. On this earth, the Holy Spirit, the energy of love, is always celebrating a liturgy of praise. This ever-recurring liturgical act is comprised of all that nature shows us—seasons, growth, death, new life, rainbows, storms—each with its own unique form of beauty. The world of nature presents us with a variegated splendor greater than any we can imagine, a pageant of divine life all around us. Adoration is our way of responding to this epiphany of God in matter. Our adoration is not simply an action on our part. It is a hymn to the delicate beauty of the cosmos, a recognition of its exquisite holiness. We keep noticing that all of nature is nothing less than an ostensorium that perpetually displays God's presence.

Adoration is directly related to beauty, what attracts our awe and devotion. The beauty of the universe is a mirror image of what abides in our own souls. George Tavard writes, "At the acme of mystical experience, the world of nature is reintegrated into divine beauty."[2] St. John himself wrote in the *Spiritual Canticle* that the Beloved, Christ, passing through the groves "left them, by his glance alone, clothed in beauty."[3] In all this, we see the connection between adoration and an impassioned love of the earth.

Adoring is also a way of entering a divine presence in a *feeling* way. That feeling leads us to a love that keeps expanding to include the entire cosmos, the mystical body of God. Adoration is the link between worship and love. Making this awe-filled connection leads us to behold and tread the earth in an aura of reverence and wonder.

Yes, love is wooing us to itself through all created life. We bring our adoring attitude to that life, the divine within all things. Love is gathering all of us into unity. Such love can become palpable to us in moments of adoration when we feel a oneness with all the people on earth—and all earthly things—who are adoring with us. Thus, the result of our adoration is our becoming a loving communion, one life, one body, one being.

Teilhard recognized oneness as "the disappearance of the alleged barrier that separates the Within of things from the Without" (HM, 27). In all phenomena is a noumenon, a divine spark in the flint of the material world, an implicit reality under what is explicit, an invisible spirit under everything visible, a limitlessness under everything limited, an unbroken wholeness under everything fragmented, a universal consciousness under everything individual, a new life, the risen life of Christ, in every ending. We are adoring the divine life in all its elegant manifestations.

Mystical consciousness is a unitive consciousness, our sense of oneness. As we saw above, there is no "I adore this," only "adoration is happening." The earth is adoring the God within it, and we are invited to join in. Teilhard approaches it this way in a letter written in 1916: "Besides communion with God and communion with the Earth, is there a communion with God through the Earth—the Earth becoming like a great Host in which God would be contained for us?"[4]

Teilhard promises that we will draw "strength" from "the enduring powers of nature." We find that strength when we turn toward the divine in matter in all its manifold vicissitudes. We can return to the metaphor of seasons to understand this more clearly. They represent the earth's reliable and enduring surrender to change. This change seems like an ending, but it is a cycle of life through death to renewal. It seems that the lily is gone, but its life beyond death is buried in the earth and its bulb will bloom again next year. It seems that winter kills off all the colors in nature, but only to present more subtle ones that will soon turn to brighter ones again.

Now we come to see how we can adore *with* nature: Our surrender to the fact of change, our practice of the unconditional yes to life as it is, becomes a faith-building attitude of adoration. Nature shows us how by its assent to change and its trust in renewal. We trust in the coming of renewal someday, even when we see no promise of it in the bleakest December of our lives. This optimism is what is meant by the virtue of hope. Our yes moves us to trust and that is faith.

We contact the powers of nature to find the strength and energy to face what happens to us. The two practices reflected in nature help us: saying yes to what is and trusting what will be. The lily says yes without protest against its dying and trusts its resurrection. We too can let go of arguing with the facts of changing and ending. We can keep saying yes and notice how that leads us to trust what will unfold. These practices of adoration join us to the earth. Together we are venerating change as well as growth. In a world where things are born and die, we are ultimately adoring a changeless reality beyond birth and death. It is therefore a defiant adoration. Living in that divine paradox of changelessness in change is what is meant by joining nature in its endless anthem of adoration.

> *Although we practice with people, our goal is to practice with mountains and rivers, with trees and stones, with everything in the world, everything in the universe, and to find ourselves in this big cosmos.... [Then] we know intuitively which way to go.*

> —Shunryu Suzuki, *Not Always So*

Prayer

I adore the You in all the galaxies. I join them in adoring You.

I adore the You in sun, and moon, and stars. I join them in adoring You.

I adore the You I see in the shifting seasons. I join them in adoring You.

I adore the You in clouds and clear skies. I join them in adoring You.

I adore the You in calm and quakes. I join them in adoring You.

I adore the You in hurricanes and rainbows. I join them in adoring You.

I adore the You in mountains, rivers, and seas. I join them in adoring You.

I adore the You in meadows and deserts. I join them in adoring You.

I adore the You in flowers and trees. I join them in adoring You.

I adore the You in all conscious beings. I join them in adoring You.

I adore the You in everything. I join everything in adoring You.

I rejoice because I adore not as one alone but as one-in-All.

FOR FURTHER REFLECTION

The fragrance of your power over me and the touch of your hand upon me…the joy of finding and surrendering to a beauty greater than us, the rapture of being possessed. (HU, 119)

I am writing these lines from an exuberance of life, a yearning to live; they are written to express an impassioned vision of the earth, and in an attempt to find a solution for the doubts that beset my action because I love the universe, its energies, its secrets, and its hopes and because at the same time I am dedicated to God, the only Origin, the only Issue, and the only Term. I want to express my love of matter and life, and to reconcile it, if possible, with the unique adoration of the only absolute and definitive Godhead. (WTW, 14)

Research is the highest form of adoration. (BE, 56)

To some, the world has disclosed itself as too vast: within such immensity, man is lost and no longer counts; and there is nothing left for him to do but shut his eyes and disappear. To others, on the contrary, the world is too beautiful; and it, and it alone, must be adored. (DM, 8)

I really feel that now I am always living in God's presence. (Teilhard's spoken words to his friend, Pierre Leroy, SJ)

The only way to make life bearable is to love and adore that which, beneath everything, animates and directs it. (LT, 227)

Lord Jesus Christ, you truly contain within your gentleness, within your humanity, all the unyielding immensity and grandeur of the world. And it is because of this, it is because there exists in you this ineffable synthesis of what our human thought and experience would never have dared join together in order to adore them—element—and totality, the one and the many, mind and matter, the infinite and the personal; it is because of the indefinable contours which this complexity gives to your appearance and to your activity, that my heart, enamored of cosmic reality, gives itself passionately to you. (HU, 73)

11

OUR CALLING
TO PLANETARY
CONSCIOUSNESS

*We cannot but recognize the objective, experiential, reality
of a transformation of the planet as a whole.*

—Pierre Teilhard de Chardin, *The Heart of Matter*

Pierre Teilhard de Chardin's work asks each of us the central
question of our lives: "What is my highest vision of what the
world needs?" He escorts us to the answer we have seen again and
again in this book: a planetary awakening, a new Pentecost. Our
part is to midwife it by being fully what we fully are: evolution
becoming personal, humans in a collective humanity, beings who
are God's Body. The world around us is, then, not just a location;
it is a calling to cosmic consciousness. God is more than one who
calls; God is the calling. The natural world and what happens in
the world are how we hear it.

In practical terms, this means that we begin to see Jesus making a bid to us in every human face, in every act of nature, and in

every world event. Our Christian commitment is aimed at saving the planet. We do this when we align ourselves with the forces of evolution that are longing passionately for more and more caring connection, what is meant to show up in our world as justice, peace, and love. These are three specific callings to us and three graces that we can receive and act on as well. Nothing can divert us once we make our commitment to a life of service to society and our planet. This is why we were given a lifetime in a world so intricately and inextricably connected. It is a connectedness that asks us to make it into a communion. How do we do this?

Our presence on earth was always meant to be a graced occasion for Christ to incarnate himself here on earth again. We recall St. Paul: "It is no longer I who live, but it is Christ who lives in me" (Gal 2:20). When we act in favor of justice, peace, and love, we give Christ one more opportunity to live another lifetime here among us. That is precisely how the incarnation continues in time. Now we see more clearly what is meant by finding God in the world of matter. Now we are struck more cogently by the mystery of how the cosmos is the mystical body of Christ. Now we are moved by how deep and lasting is the purposeful love that brought us here.

We can look at some specific planetary issues that call for our concern and action today. We can see how they become social sins when we engage in what harms our planet and its people. They are helpful actions when we take a stand for the welfare of our world:

What harms the planet and its people	What helps the planet and its people
Exploitation of the environment	Caretaking and protection of the environment

Economic injustice	Designing a political system that shares wealth and services
War and genocide	Nonviolence in all our responses to conflicts
Nuclear weapon-building	Disarmament on an international level
Slavery, human trafficking	Respect for all people, refusal to take advantage of others
Oppression based on race, gender, sexual orientation, religion, political affiliation	Acceptance of and respect for the rainbow world we live in
These represent an absence of planetary consciousness.	These represent planetary consciousness, a form of love.

There is, alongside the obviously destructive forces on our planet, a growing current that will lead to a new level of human awareness…a dimly sensed recognition that the strongest force in our universe is not overriding power, but love.

—Carl Rogers, *A Way of Being*

MEDITATION

The phrase "Sense of the Earth" should be understood to mean the passionate concern for our common destiny which draws the thinking part of life ever further onward. In principle there is no feeling which has a firm foundation in nature, or greater power. But in fact there is also no feeling which awakens so belatedly, since it can become explicit only when our consciousness has expanded beyond the broadening, but still far too restricted, circles of family, country and race, and has finally discovered that the only truly natural and real human Unity is the Spirit of Earth. (BE, 43)

Reflection

All humans long for fulfillment and completion. There is an inherent impulse in us toward Pleroma (fulfillment) and Parousia (completion). As we become more spiritually conscious, we notice them and move toward them. Since we are not alone but linked, our journey is not only for our own welfare. We are headed toward a planetary awakening, a universal Pentecost, a cosmic awakening to fulfillment of Christ's purpose and completion of Christ's work.

The paschal mystery—the death, resurrection, ascension experience of Christ and the Pentecost of the Holy Spirit—simultaneously showed us the high points of God's evolutionary work. Another example of the paschal mystery as all in one is mentioned by Teilhard in "Reflections on Original Sin": "Creation, incarnation and redemption are to be seen as no more than three complementary aspects of one and the same process." In fact, in the mystical perspective, all the events of salvation history are always happening in one and the same moment, now.

There has always been a longing in us for wholeness *and* it is already in us. Spiritual wholeness means we are holding Pleroma (fulfillment) and Parousia (completion) in our hearts. Likewise, as we saw above, our wholeness as individuals leads to a collective wholeness. Teilhard states, "It is through that which is most incommunicably personal in us that we make contact with the universal" (CE 97). Indeed, all are called, yet each in his or her own uniqueness—reminiscent of the phrase "each in his own language"

105

at Pentecost. The journey of each of us in this lifetime is from an evolved consciousness to an evolved society. Here is an extended prayer affirmation for us as individuals that combines an evolutionary spirituality with planetary awareness:

> I hold the intention of continuing to evolve and I hold the evolving world in my heart, as Jesus does.
>
> I want to contact the evolutionary impulse I have felt in me at special moments. It is an excitement about my place in the world and a compelling urge to grow into all I am here to be.
>
> Something lives in me, irreversible and ineradicable, and it wants to stretch into full spiritual adulthood. It is Christ wanting to reach the fullness of his life in the course of my life.
>
> I know this inclination is not coming from me but through me. It a grace from the Holy Spirit not based on my efforts but calling for them.
>
> I know there is an evolutionary impulse alive in all people and things not only in me. I know I can rely on the grace to let it flourish in me and to share it so that all beings can come along with me.

We are walking together on a Camino to the fullness of Christ. The joy of this realization leads me to a commitment to the welfare of all humanity and the planet that holds us all. We hear Teilhard join us in this realization as he asks us, "No longer, as in the past, for our small selves, for our small family, our small country; but for the salvation and the success of the universe, how must we, modern people, organize around us for the best, the maintenance, distribution and progress of human energy?" (BE, 67).

Finally, a planetary consciousness also leads to gratitude. We realize that the whole cosmos is involved in our surviving and thriving. The sun makes food possible. The moon makes tides possible. All nature acts in harmony. A calling speaks through analogy. Thus, in a natural mysticism, our calling is to do what nature does, nurture all beings and find harmony with them. Likewise, nature always combines continuity and variety, something abides while something changes. This too is an analogy for our calling. We stay loyal to our standards of caring connection, and we keep finding new ways to show it. We hold fast to our commitment to acting with justice, peace, and love. We also never give up looking for new and different ways to do this.

- Today and daily, we work for planetary goals; we take a stand against earth depredation.
- Today and daily, we awaken as individuals who care about the awakening of our human collective.
- Today and daily, we are thankful for the grace that blessed us with planetary awareness.

With this awareness we find the grace of courage in ourselves. We will no longer be afraid of what happens to us and around us on this, at times, frightening globe. What happens will be Christ appearing in world events. He walks toward us on the waves and assures us: "Take heart, *it* is *I*; do not be afraid" (Matt 14:27, emphases added). In mystical nonduality, everything we take to be an "it"—outside us and coming at us—is actually an "I"—part of us. This "I" does not refer to ego. Faith in divine presence makes every it a "You." Once we open ourselves to mystical consciousness, we feel that God is everything real and what makes everything real. Then reality is personal, a You, God present in all that is and through all that happens. This is how planetary consciousness leads to freedom from the fear that we are ever alone.

We never are deserted quite.
—Christopher Smart, "On a Bed of Guernsey Lilies"

Prayer
(Based on the Preface for the Mass of Pentecost)

May we always and everywhere give You thanks,
Fatherly and Motherly God, for how tenderly You care for
us and our world.
Our hearts are burning within us as we celebrate a
planetary Pentecost in our world here and now.
You completed the paschal mystery and sent Your Holy Spirit
to unite us and all creation in the Heart of Your Son.
This same Spirit gave birth to Your Church, the
community called to limitless love for all people and for
all our planet.
We are thankful to the Holy Spirit for opening us to
Your ongoing invitation to cocreate, with You and one
another, a world of justice, peace, and love.
We honor the Holy Spirit by joining with all peoples in one
act of hope for and commitment to the earth.
Now, vibrant with paschal joy, every land, every people,
every being exults in praising and thanking You.
We can even hear the angels singing with us in one never-
ending hymn to Your glory:

Holy, Holy, Holy Lord God of hosts.
Heaven and earth are full of Your glory.
Hosanna in the highest.
Blessed is He who comes in the name of the Lord.
Hosanna in the highest.

FOR FURTHER REFLECTION

To have access to the divine milieu is to have found the one thing
needful: him who burns by setting fire to everything that we would

love badly or not enough; him who calms by eclipsing with his blaze everything that we would love too much; him who consoles by gathering up everything that has been snatched from our love or has never been given to it. To reach those priceless layers is to experience, with equal truth, that one has need of everything, and that one has need of nothing. Everything is needed because the world will never be large enough to provide our taste for action with the means of grasping God, or our thirst for undergoing with the possibility of being invaded by him. And yet nothing is needed; for as the only reality which can satisfy us lies beyond the transparencies in which it is mirrored, everything that fades away and dies between us will only serve to give reality back to us with greater purity. Everything means both everything and nothing to me; everything is God to me and everything is dust to me: that is what man can say with equal truth, in accord with how the divine ray falls. (DM, 92)

[This], above all, is the message I wish to communicate: the reconciliation of God and the world because it reconciles God and the world. (WTW, 18)

When the signs of age begin to mark my body, Lord, (and still more when they mark my mind), when the illness that is to diminish me or carry me off strikes from without, or is born within me; when the painful moment comes in which I suddenly awaken to the fact that I am ill or growing old, and above all, at that last moment, when I feel I am losing hold of myself and am absolutely passive within the hands of the great unknown forces that have formed me. (DM, 57)

Grant, when my hour comes, that I may recognize you under the species of each alien or hostile force that seems bent upon destroying or uprooting me....In all those dark moments, O God, grant that I may understand that it is you who are painfully parting the fibers of my being in order to penetrate to the very marrow of my substance and bear me away within yourself....Teach me to treat my death as an act of communion. (OS, 82)

Above all, trust in the slow work of God. We are quite naturally impatient in everything to reach the end without delay. We should like to skip the intermediate stages. We are impatient of being on the way to something unknown, something new. And yet it is the law of all progress that it is made by passing through some stages of instability—and that it may take a very long time. And so I think it is with you; your ideas mature gradually—let them grow, let them shape themselves, without undue haste. Don't try to force them on, as though you could be today what time (that is to say, grace and circumstances acting on your own good will) will make of you tomorrow. Only God could say what this new spirit gradually forming within you will be. Give Our Lord the benefit of believing that his hand is leading you, and accept the anxiety of feeling yourself in suspense and incomplete. (Letter to his cousin, Marguerite)

At a time when the consciousness of its own powers and possibilities is legitimately awakening in humankind, now ready to become adult, one of the first duties of a Christian is to show, by the logic of his religious views and still more by the logic of his actions, that the incarnate God did not come to diminish in us the glorious responsibility and splendid ambition that is ours: to fashion our own self. *Non munuit, sed sacravit* [he did not make less but made sacred]. (DM, 34)

12

SHINING FUTURE, GLOWING EXPECTANCY

I am a pilgrim of the future on my way back from a journey made entirely in the past.

—Teilhard de Chardin, *Letters from a Traveller*

In the early Church, people expected the second coming of Christ to happen in their lifetime. As the centuries passed and the Church became more institutionalized, the hierarchy moved away from that focus. The Christian calling was to be about individual salvation rather than preparation for a collective apocalypse that would happen soon.

Teilhard lamented that our sense of expectancy about the coming of the reign of Christ is now well-nigh gone: "Only twenty centuries have passed since the Ascension. What have we made of our expectancy?...How many of us are genuinely moved in the depths of our hearts by the wild hope that our earth will be recast?... Where is the Catholic as passionately vowed (by conviction not by convention) to spreading the dream of a new city? We persist in saying that we keep vigil in expectation of the Master. But in reality we should have to admit, if we were sincere, that we no longer expect anything" (DM, 131).

An evolutionary spirituality recovers the sense of expectancy about the future. We become aware of God beckoning to us not from the past but from ahead in the future. As we have noted, God is the ahead, the future awaiting us, the coming "one" as in the word *oneness*, universal consciousness.

For Teilhard, the primacy of Spirit correlates directly with the primacy of the future. Our faith in the Holy Spirit makes us aware, expectant, welcoming, and caring about what is to come.

The second coming is usually thought of as "the end of time," a moment that will usher in the "world to come." In mystical consciousness, we speak not of the world to come but of a world always becoming. Christ is always entering time, not en route to ending it, but to animate it, to set it on fire. This is not the fire of destruction but the fire of ignition. We are welcoming in a new world, a new way of being in the world, a new destiny in the world.

We hope for a world with a peace room rather than a war room; with equality rather than oppression and injustice; with love rather than division; with caring for our planet rather than leaving a footprint of greed, hate, and ignorance.

Yet, we remain aware of the shadow side in each of us and in the human collective. The dark side figures into how we see the future and experience our sense of expectancy. The second coming is indeed often associated with a onetime cataclysm aimed at the elimination of evil: "And war broke out in heaven; Michael and his angels fought against the dragon. The dragon and his angels fought back, but they were defeated, and there was no longer any place for them in heaven....Then I heard a loud voice in heaven, proclaiming, 'Now have come the salvation and the power / and the kingdom of our God / and the authority of his Messiah'"

(Rev 12:7–8, 10). This is the coming of Christ as the Messiah of a new order. The second coming will produce not worldwide destruction but "salvation and the power and the kingdom of our God." Thus, our collective hope is in a new way of being human, a trust in universal salvation. We will then seek power for justice instead of power for domination. We will live in a world designed by light, not by darkness. The coming of the Christ we expect is a promise of renewal of the human race.

We are aware of how the forces of darkness keep making appearances. They do not go away, but faith assures us they will not have the last word. What does this mean? In his words about death, Origen helps us understand the analogy to evil: "Its destruction, therefore, will not mean that it no longer exists, but that it ceases to be an enemy….For nothing is…incapable of restoration to its Creator. He made all things that they might exist, and those things which were made for existence cannot cease to be."[1] Our hope is in continuous restoration of goodness not in total elimination of evil. Some battles are won by evil; the final victory is always that of love. Gandhi, in *The Law of Love*, notes, "I have found that life persists in the midst of destruction and, therefore, there must be a higher law than that of destruction."

In mystical devotion, the coming of Christ is also about how he enters our lives personally, meeting us heart-to-heart. This happens not at a day in the future that we are waiting for but in any moment of any day. It happens not in a trumpet blast of gigantic proportion but in simplicity and human warmth. This version of the coming of Christ is described in the "I will come in" expressed so touchingly in another part of the Book of Revelation. We hear Christ inviting us individually to his messianic banquet: "Listen! I am standing at the door, knocking; if you hear my voice and open the door, I will come in to you and eat with you, and you with me" (Rev 3:20). That coming of Christ is awaiting us right now and continues to do so without end. All we have to say is "Yes, come, Lord Jesus."

Love came as a guest
Into my heart,
My soul then opened,
So that love could dine in me.

—Ibn Hazm, Islamic mystic, "Ring of the Dove"

MEDITATION

The more the future opens before me like some dizzy abyss or dark tunnel, the more confident I may be—if I venture forward on the strength of your word—of losing myself and surrendering myself in you, of being assimilated by your body, Jesus. (HU, 105)

Reflection

Teilhard suggests that we "will learn again to expect" (DM, 133) when we meet the future with the inventiveness of the present. In a fully embodied spirituality, we find ways to use science, electronics, natural resources, financials, and technologies for good. They help us usher the future, effectively and nonviolently, into our contemporary world. We find ways to use our manifold resources for love not division, with wisdom not ignorance.

Teilhard does not propose a linear path to the future. He uses the word "ascending." We are spiraling upward into a higher consciousness, a more mature sense of who we are and who God is, a more passionate zeal for connection with the divine through matter. Teilhard trusted in a continual ascension to wholeness. Our expectancy blooms with excitement when we see the future this way. It is no longer about the time to come but rather about *how we become*.

This evolutionary arc is not elitist. The portal into the future "will open only to an advance of all together" (PM, 244). Our spiral dance into the future is a collective venture, all for one and one for all. We carry all beings with us: "The only reward for my labor I now covet is to be able to think that it is being used for the essential and lasting progress of the universe" (WTW, 42).

Rising into the future of light can only be a cosmic ascent after all. To say that the gates of the future are open to us is an example of global awareness. When Teilhard muses that the age of the nations is long gone, he asks what Pope Francis is asking in *Laudato Si'*—that we join in saving, caretaking, and building the earth as a place of friendliness toward and safety for all peoples. Societies based on violence and exclusion are opposing the new future ruled by justice, peace, and love. Our only chance is an earthwide consciousness and limitless caring connection. This is how our mystical sense of oneness manifests at a planetary level, the only level that can accommodate it.

The horizons of the future we seek, the same future Jesus sought, are not yet clearly in view. In fact, they remain, as Teilhard says, "ever more shrouded in mist" (CE, 132). This is where we meet the great challenge of trusting that there really is a kingdom coming, that there really is a risen Christ piloting it into existence. We are certainly not encouraged about the new heaven and the new earth when we hear of terrorism, injustice, and oppression each day in the news. There seems to be no room for anything beyond viciousness and hate.

Our indomitable trust that evil can't win, that darkness can't overcome, has two implications. Both are challenges to our faith:

- Our expectancy for the kingdom of Christ and the triumph of goodness on earth are justified.
- No matter how grueling the challenge we will have to face, there will always be grace to match and meet it.

Teilhard tells us how to "triumph *over* the world" of death and destruction. We will pray that Christ will "come to us clothed in the glory *of* the world" (DM, 102). This is a profound paradox to live by. Only our joining Jesus Christ as people deeply immersed in the world, with all its suffering and darkness, equips us to halt humanity's trudge toward annihilation. This is how we inaugurate its march to renewal. We are here on earth because this is where incarnation is, this is where redemption happens, this is the true focus of our life and destiny.

Many of us were taught about salvation history with an undue emphasis on the past. We were dismayed by how our first parents' sin hobbled our chances for happiness. We were lucky that Christ came many centuries later to save us from our wounded selves. We can now think of Christ's mission as more than rescue from the sin in Eden. He came here because he loves being with us and for us, and he is still here. His loving purpose is so far-reaching that the glories he launched are still not fully known to us. We can trust the Holy Spirit to enlighten us today and any day in a Pentecostal fire with a universal blaze: "But the Advocate, the Holy Spirit, whom the Father will send in my name, will teach you everything, and remind you of all that I have said to you" (John 14:26).

Our new sense of life is about a future being born anew each day. Our world, in Teilhard's view, is not static. It is still being born from its conception almost fourteen billion years ago. The promise in salvation history thus goes beyond repairing the past: "I am making all things new" (Rev 21:5). Evolution itself is a promise. It represents reliable hope since it always both promises and delivers a more conscious and caring connection—what we need to thrive both physically and spiritually. We have this lifetime to let Christ evolve within our human family. We have a future so we can keep "being assimilated by" his body, our evolving universe. This means committing ourselves to his new kingdom, a society built on a conscious and loving connection.

In his Sermon on the Mount, Jesus describes the kingdom to come, the future we are here to welcome, the commitment we are here to keep: we commit ourselves to love our enemies, to do good to those who hate us, to bless those who curse us, to pray for those who mistreat us. The Sermon on the Mount is radical because it defies the worldly style of aggression, domination, and vengeance in favor of gentle love as the more powerful alternative. Observing these teachings from the Sermon on the Mount allows the coming of Christ to happen in us both individually and collectively.

Mystical spirituality thus has to be embodied in behavior based on what the Sermon recommends. This behavior moves us from the Golgatha of our present sufferings to a new Jerusalem.

Prayer
(Based on the Sermon on the Mount)

Jesus, by the help of Your grace,
I commit myself to love my enemies, to do good to those
*   who hate me, to bless those who curse me, to pray for*
*   those who mistreat me.*
Let me be merciful, as Your heavenly Father is merciful.
Let me not judge others but accept them with
*   understanding and compassion.*
Let me not condemn anyone but look for the goodness in
*   everyone.*
Let me forgive as I am forgiven.
Let me be generous and thankful for all Your generosity
*   toward me.*
Let me grow in social awareness and keep evolving in
*   spiritual fervor.*
Let me be joyful in hope, patient in difficulties, faithful in
*   prayer.*
Let me rejoice with those who rejoice; mourn with those
*   who mourn.*
Let me live in harmony with everyone.

Let me not be overcome by evil, but overcome evil with good.
Jesus, by all these commitments, I am welcoming in the dazzling future You planned for our world.

FOR FURTHER REFLECTION

Why, before I act, should I be concerned to know whether my effort will be noticed or appreciated? Why should I feed my appetite for action with the empty hope of prestige or popularity? The only reward for my labor I now covet is to be able to think that it is being used for the essential and lasting progress of the universe. (WTW, 42)

The Age of Nations is past. The task before us now, if we would not perish, is to build the Earth....We have reached a crossroads in human evolution where the only road which leads forward is towards a common passion....To continue to place our hopes in a social order achieved by external violence would simply amount to our giving up all hope of carrying the Spirit of the Earth to its limits. (BE, 54)

Is not precisely the whole course of centuries needed in order for our gaze to accustom itself to the light?...I am prepared to press on to the end along a path on which each step makes me more certain, toward horizons that are ever more shrouded in mist. (CE, 132)

Only he who has fought bravely and been victorious in the struggle against the spurious security and strength and attraction of the past can attain to the firm and blissful experiential certainty that the more we lose all foothold in the darkness and instability of the future, the more deeply we penetrate into God. (HU, 136)

The more I prayed, the more deeply did God materialize for me in a reality that was at once spiritual and tangible. In that reality, the great synthesis was beginning to be effected in which my life would be summed up: the synthesis of the above with the ahead. (HM, 44)

The expectation of heaven cannot remain alive unless it is incarnate. What body shall we give to ours today? That of a huge and totally human hope. (DM, 132)

Disperse, O Jesus, the clouds with your lightning! Show yourself to us as the Mighty, the Radiant, the Risen! Come to us once again as the Pantocrator who filled the solitude of the cupolas in the ancient basilicas! Nothing less than this Parousia is needed to counter-balance and dominate in our hearts the glory of the world that is coming into view. And so that we should triumph over the world with you, come to us clothed in the glory of the world. (DM, 102)

13

INFINITE TREASURES OF GRACE

The grace of God can convert hearts and offer mankind a
way out of humanly insoluble situations.

—Pope Francis, Christmas Message, 2015

Grace is how God helps and supports us on our journey through life. Grace is what gives us more courage, more wisdom, more love than our ego could ever summon up on its own. Grace gives us access to the More within us, that is, the indwelling Holy Spirit: "Not by might, nor by power, but by my spirit, says the LORD of hosts" (Zech 4:6). The experience of grace coming to us in so many ways on so many days shows us we are never alone.

In the New Testament, we find many references to grace and its powers: Grace is a calling (see 2 Tim 1:9; Gal 1:15); has saving power (see Eph 2:5); makes us holy (see Rom 3:24; Titus 3:7); moves our focus away from effort and the following of laws as the only path to salvation (see Rom 6:14; Heb 10:4; John 1:17); can be shared through preaching the word (see Eph 3:8); came to us in Jesus Christ (see John 1:17); is reliable and sufficient as we face life's challenges (see 2 Cor 12:9); comes to us in and as a revelation (see 1 Pet 1:13); is always available to us (see Rom 5:1–2); and is our true teacher (see Titus 2:11–12).

Grace is a free gift, so it is not parceled out to us on the basis of efforts or merits. (We can be glad to know that!) We cannot make grace happen or earn it, but we can open ourselves to it. We do this by our yes to what is, by prayer, and by a continuous sense of gratitude. We open to grace also when we use the graces we receive in the service of others and of our world. Grace has one ultimate purpose, to make us more like Christ. We manifest this likeness by acts of love. Grace is how God shows love to us; loving others is how we show thanks to God for grace.

We are in the world not like an albatross around the neck of God. We are here instead as the beloved disciple resting on the Heart of Jesus. Nothing we have ever done has lessened God's love for us. We see this in the endless access we have to grace, no matter how far from the spiritual path we have wandered.

What makes God so enamored of us? Why does God give us grace so bounteously? It is not our trophies, our conquests, our successes that attract grace. It is our vulnerability, our brokenness, our penchant for mistakes, our compromises of conscience, our failures at adhering to our calling, our longing for love but seeking it in places that can't provide it. God is sympathetic to our missing the point. Indeed, Jesus knows better than us how hard it is to be human.

Grace shows us that God—limitless love—is touched by our misled longings, moved by our failings, drawn to our wayward inclinations. This is why humble recognition of the power of grace in our lives is the path to God. St. Therese of Lisieux reminds us, "That is precisely the cause of my joy; since I have nothing, I shall expect everything from the good God....Jesus wants to grant us the same graces, wants to give us His Heaven as a free gift."[1] Likewise, we recall St. Paul: "He [God] said to me, 'My grace is sufficient for you, for power is made perfect in weakness.' So, I will boast all the more gladly of my weaknesses, so that the power of Christ may dwell in me" (2 Cor 12:9). God looks not for great deeds but great openness to grace.

Grace is the life of God in us, how God is close. That might scare us at times; our fears of intimacy are not only directed at people with whom we are in relationship. We have the same two fears about God that we have about persons: We sometimes fear closeness—God too near. We sometimes fear abandonment— God too far. Jesus living in us by grace releases us from any fear of God's nearness. Jesus feeling forsaken on the cross releases us from terror about his abandonment. His life in us is freedom from fear. Grace is the key to that freedom, a key being placed in our hands here and now.

Grace might also scare us because it calls on us to be in the world as God is, one who gives without stinting. We actually have nothing to fear; grace engenders in us an impulse toward generosity. That virtue can feel threatening to the ego, so self-concerned. Yet grace is humbling too so that our ego might take a bow. We will then notice more ability to share precisely because of what we have received.

Finally, "grace given by God" can sound dualistic. In mystical consciousness, grace is not a dollop of spiritual sweetener bestowed from above. It is an animating force that enriches us from deep within and from all around. We note the following encouragement given in a homily in 2013 by Pope Francis: "Submit to the Holy Spirit that *comes from within us* and makes [us] go forward along the path of holiness."[2] That is grace, coming from within and moving us forward. We access a courage to face more, a wisdom to understand more, a love to open ourselves more. That courage, wisdom, and love is directed not only to people who are nearby. Grace is always both personal and universal, and extends also to our caring for the planet.

MEDITATION

Through grace, through that single and identical life, we become much more than kinsmen, much more, even, than brothers: we become identified with one and the same higher Reality, which is Jesus Christ. (WTW, 50)

Reflection

Our spiritual life is a harmony of achieving and receiving. We seek to achieve spiritual progress when we act with integrity and love, when we perform spiritual practices. Yet, there is more to holiness, more to our awakening. We also need grace as the gift that gives us perseverance on our spiritual path. We engage in our practices precisely *because* we are touched by grace. Thus, grace is necessary through and through for a whole spirituality to flourish. We ask for grace without expectation because it is a gift. We turn to it with expectancy because it is so available.

There is a light that comes to us when we first awaken to the glory of God in all that is. That is the grace of beginning a spiritual path. Grace activates us. Then we live in gratitude for grace and see it everywhere in our experience and in our world. Next, we want to share the gift we have found. We become devoted to spreading the good news. We share the fire of our passion for God's kingdom "in ever widening circles, until finally the whole planet is suffused in light" (PM, 182).

We thus do not request grace only for ourselves. We ask for the grace of being a light to the world around us. We ask that all people become aware of the graces that are always available to them. We are also asking that grace touches the hearts of those who are wounding the earth and its peoples. Such bigness in our prayer and spiritual attitude is itself a gift of grace.

We are pleased to see evolution always moving in an arc of ascent. This is not just a scientific datum, it is also a gift of grace to humanity. We contribute to the positive direction of evolution when we make daily decisions for environmental survival. This will not feel like a chore. Evolution is already stirring in us, moving us forward—grace at work in our human nature. Grace calls us to join the advancing direction, what happens in our contemplation when it is animated with an apostolic intent.

All the news and history of our world is offering us an opportunity to join in the incarnational project of world Christification. We are being given the grace to join as *prophets*. Spirituality is prophetic in two senses. First, we become wise commentators on how what happens can have a Christic dimension; second, we look for ways to bring Christ's Heart and message into world events.

Most of us will not have the worldly power to make the enormous changes required, but we can join in projects that make some difference. This means that we begin to think of ourselves as actors on the world stage, even in bit parts, even behind the scenes, even if all we can invest is prayer, time, and money. To speak up in any way about policies that harm the planet and to support planetary survival is how our spirituality becomes truly prophetic in action. We will also trust that grace is always at work in the world no matter who is in charge and no matter how dire the nightly news.

Graces will come our way to give us the wisdom and courage to fulfill our divine mission. Every calling can be trusted to come with corresponding graces to help us fulfill it. Our prophetic voice is boosted by grace no matter how faint. Our faith commitment to today's world is thus ultimately a trust in the power of grace. It is not scarce; it is abundant: "I came that they may have life, and have it abundantly" (John 10:10).

The birth of evolution is the Big Bang, the first burst of grace to humanity—what is meant by "life, and have it abundantly." In mystical awareness, the Christ who is incarnate in the world of matter is not only the Pantocrator, the ruler archetype. The incarnate Christ is also Jesus at birth, vulnerable yet powerful, as

Teilhard reminds us: "The mystical Christ, the Universal Christ of
St. Paul has neither meaning nor value in our eyes except as an
expression of the Christ who was born of Mary" (DM, 89).

As we ponder the mystery of grace in the Christmas mystery,
we see Jesus in the arms of Mary. Ongoing incarnation means that
the divine feminine, creative and nurturant power, is holding Christ
and, on this very day, is presenting him to angels, shepherds, and
kings. The nativity scene, which we are all so familiar with, pro-
vides a powerful spiritual image to live by. *Grace is the greatness of
God come to smallness.* The mystery of Christmas portrays the divine
in the lowliest human state. We see the all-powerful in the power-
less. Grace shows us that the strongest force is the most defenseless.
This is precisely the paradox of grace: help comes to us without
regard for stature, strength, or accomplishment. The infant Jesus is
the symbol of this magnificent paradox in the story of us and grace.

Yahweh came to us as a burning bush, unapproachable. Zeus
came in thunderbolts, intimidating. Our God came as a needy,
poor, and helpless infant, the most nonthreatening form of arrival,
not only approachable but embraceable. The other gods came into
the world making demands on us. Ours comes in needing us.

Jesus lies in a lowly manger, a foreigner in a foreign town, as
a needy, poor, and helpless infant, the most nonthreatening form
of arrival, not only approachable but embraceable. This state of
rejection, displacement, and poverty is a metaphor for how Christ
is present in our world today. He is the unwanted and penniless
immigrant, the refugee, the exile. We cannot let the grandeur of
the cosmic Christ obscure what he looks like in his Christmas
reality: a poor stowaway in an unwelcoming world. By the grace
of universal love, we will see our God in the many thousands of
faces that look like his on our planet today. God not only sent, he
came. God not only came, he stayed. God stays on earth not only
in the eucharistic bread but in the breadless poor.

Christ at the nativity, symbol of the grace of birth, also shows
us that the crises of our time do not have to hurl us into despair.

They are the pangs of new birth: "We know that the whole creation has been groaning in labor pains until now" (Rom 8:22). This verse from St. Paul pulls together our theme of grace and the infant Jesus as the appropriate image for the evolutionary incarnation happening in today's world.

> There are really only two ways, it seems to me, in which we can think about our existence here on Earth. We either agree with Macbeth that life is nothing more than a "tale told by an idiot," a purposeless emergence of life-forms including the clever, greedy, selfish, and unfortunately destructive species that we call *Homo sapiens*—the "evolutionary goof." Or we believe that, as Pierre Teilhard de Chardin put it, "There is something afoot in the universe, something that looks like gestation and birth." In other words, a plan, a purpose to it all.[3]

Prayer

Infant Jesus, give me the grace to know how to be born, how to come alive for humanity.

Show me how to turn to Your Mother, how to find comfort and empowerment in her arms.

Show me how to hold the world in my arms. Make my arms wide enough to embrace the whole of humanity, good and evil alike, with limitless love.

You care deeply about those whose hell it is to hate and hurt.

You came into the world as a hunted person, an object of derision and hate.

May I respond to the grace of courage to speak up for those who are hunted, tortured, and hated.

*May I have compassion too for those who hunt down,
    torture, and kill.*
*May I hear Your call to oppose and yet win over those who
    seek to destroy the planet You came to redeem.*
*Show me how to present myself to the high and mighty, the
    low and lowly, with Your promise that love not power is
    the only hope for our planet.*
*I trust in Your divine birthing power more than in any
    strategy of violence or retribution.*
*I commit myself to nonviolent love, the love You taught me
    and give me the grace to show in my every relationship
    and action.*
*I feel You in my heart right now as the source of every
    grace I need.*
*I thank You for being born in the world I am in and with
    the same human body I have.*
*I know I am being birthed daily to further Your reign,
    Prince of Peace.*

FOR FURTHER REFLECTION

A glow ripples outward from the first spark of conscious reflection. The point of ignition grows larger and the fire spreads in ever-widening circles, until finally the whole planet is suffused in light. (PM, 182)

There is an ascent of life that is invincible. (PM, 109)

When every certainty is shaken and every utterance falters, when every principle appears doubtful, then there is only one ultimate belief on which we can base our rudderless interior life: the belief that there is an absolute direction of growth, to which both our duty and our happiness demand that we align; and that life advances in that direction. (WTW, 31–32)

EVERYTHING ABLAZE

Jesus you are the center in which all things meet and which stretches out over all things. I love you for the extensions of your body and soul to the farthest corners of creation through grace, through life, and through matter. (WTW, 70)

Energy, then, becomes Presence. (HM, 99)

Through the incarnation God descended into nature in order to super-animate and take it back to him. ("The Mysticism of Science")

There is something afoot in the universe, something that looks like gestation and birth. (HU, 93)

CONCLUSION

*I shall savor, with heightened consciousness, the intense
yet tranquil rapture of a vision whose coherence and
harmonies I can never exhaust.*

—Pierre Teilhard de Chardin, "Mass on the World"

There are two mysteries we have encountered continually
throughout this book: the mystery of oneness and the
mystery of God. In conclusion, let us now look at each of these
with Teilhard's mystical perspective. In both we find "coherence
and harmonies."

A sense of oneness is essential to mysticism. Teilhard wrote,
"Somehow or other, there must be a single energy operating in the
world" (PM, 63). Here are words of Teilhard, gathered from this book,
demonstrating how he recognized a oneness in all that is: God, ourselves, matter, spirit, Christ, the Eucharist, the Sacred Heart, everything. Each statement can be used as the basis for meditation:

"Energy, then, becomes Presence" (HM, 99).
"To live the cosmic life is to live dominated by the
consciousness that one is an atom in the body of the
mystical and cosmic Christ" (WTW, 70).
"Christ has a cosmic body that extends throughout the
universe" (WTW, 58).

"I firmly believe that everything around me is the body and
blood of the Word" (HU, 21).
"The world is the final, and the real, Host into which Christ
gradually descends" (SC, 65).
"Everything is God to me and everything is dust to me"
(DM, 93).
"That, above all, is the message I wish to communicate: the
reconciliation of God and the world because it reconciles
God and the world" (WTW, 18).

Regarding the second theme, the mystery of God, while we
acknowledge that God is a mystery, in mystical consciousness,
nonetheless, we dance closer and closer to the heart of the mysterious fire. Here are some quotations about God, all from the text of
this book, that approach the mystery—and may lead to meditation:

"God is love."
"God is limitless love."
"God is oneness."
"God is opportunity for love in all that happens."
"God is the center of all that is."
"God is the being of all that is."
"God is our true nature."
"God is the real 'Who' in 'Who am I?'"
"God is everything real and what makes everything real."
"God is the here and now, the reality of this moment."
"God is what does not end."
"God is an abiding accompaniment."
"God is the ahead, the future awaiting us."
"God is fire."
"God is all yes."

Love animates and upholds our belief in oneness and in God.
We have noted how Teilhard envisioned a human community of

love as the foundation, origin, driver, and destiny of evolution. We join consciously into the process of evolution when we show universal love. For Teilhard, love was an energy, not a feeling. Indeed, love, like every energy, is ever-renewing, not passing. Love begins in attraction, moves toward greater and deeper connection, then goes beyond itself to universality and unconditionality. This is *agape*, the self-giving love referred to in the phrase "God is love." It is the true Omega point of evolution. It is this *agape* love, alive by grace in each of us, toward which all is always converging.

Teilhard de Chardin, scientist, priest, and prophet, gifted us with an encouraging earth mysticism. Ursula King wrote, "His deepest desire was to see the essence of things, to find their heart, and probe into the mystery of life, its origin and goal. In the rhythm of life and its evolution, at the center of the cosmos and the world, Teilhard believed, is a divine center, a living heart beating with the fiery energy of love and compassion."[1] Meditating on Teilhard's words, praying with him, contemplating his vision in these pages has, hopefully, moved us to have that same heart in ourselves. It is the Heart in Jesus, the one that makes all one, the one that sets everything ablaze.

> *The day will come when, after harnessing space, the winds, the tides, and gravitation, we shall harness for God the energies of love. And on that day, for the second time in the history of the world, we shall have discovered fire.*

> —Teilhard de Chardin, *Toward the Future*

APPENDIX

The Heart of Mysticism

The word *mystical* is used often in this book. We are now familiar with Teilhard's unique mysticism of nature and evolution. We find mystics from diverse religious and spiritual backgrounds, yet the qualities of mystical experience are strikingly similar.

Mysticism is a way of knowing spiritual realities by experience. Mystical experience is nondual: God, we, and all things as one infinite reality. We see God everywhere, in everything and everyone, in every moment.

Oneness does not refer to a number; it is more accurately nonnumeral than nondual. Oneness refers to a single reality, yet it includes wide-ranging diversity. Since realities are separate in our brain—and in the dictionary—we imagine they must also be separate in the world. Mystical consciousness cancels out this illusion. This does not mean that all is identical, but that all is more than simply united; it is a unity.

Mystical consciousness is also an unmediated, unbroken, direct, intimate union with God. Unmediated means beyond the need for information from our logical brain or theological authorities.

Mystical consciousness has left the precincts both of subjective thought and blind obedience. It tiptoes instead into the palace of heart, soul, and bodymind. This happens through intuition, visions, images, dreams, peak experiences, contemplation, ecstatic states, and epiphanies.

We understand mysticism more clearly when we distinguish two styles of spiritual awareness: apophatic and cataphatic. The word *apophatic* combines Greek words meaning "speak" and "off." In mystical theology, this experience is called "the negative path" to truth. On this path, we know God by way of what God is *not* rather than by how God is defined. In his "Catechetical Homilies," St. Cyril of Jerusalem said, "We explain not what God is but candidly confess that we have no exact knowledge concerning Him. For in what concerns God to confess our ignorance is the best knowledge."[1]

The accent in an apophatic, mystical knowledge of God therefore is on individual experience of the divine rather than on logic. We know but our knowledge is beyond the possibility or necessity of words. The apophatic path goes in the opposite direction than that of dogmatic certainty. This fits with St. Augustine's apophatic dictum: "If you can comprehend it, it is not God."[2]

The apophatic style is not limited to Christianity. It is what in Buddhism is called the "don't know mind." Likewise, in the thirteenth century, Moses Maimonides from the Jewish tradition wrote, "Describing God by means of negations is correct....The more negations there are regarding God, the nearer you come to apprehending God."[3]

In contrast to an apophatic style of spiritual awareness, cataphatic focuses on statements *about* God, that is, what we can know. Cataphatic is the style of theology; apophatic is the style of mysticism. Both are useful in their own ways. The apophatic orientation is how faith opens through experience, beyond the need for intellectual understanding. Indeed, faith is the opposite of knowing; it is believing without knowing. The cataphatic orientation is how faith seeks understanding while not expecting a final formulation of who God is. The two approaches complement one another.

Mystics avoid theological arguments or the need to reach final dogmatic clarity. They are comfortable with uncertainty, paradox, and metaphor. They long for more wisdom rather than more exact descriptions of beliefs. They give up the need to know—ultimately an attempt to be in control—for awareness, a choice to be open.

Some mystics use the word *revelations* to describe their personal realizations. In the mystical view, revelation is ongoing and personal rather than limited to or ended by official pronouncements. Thus, what comes to them from their contemplation of a teaching *is* a teaching. Doctrine is a springboard to the mystic, not a final landing. Hindu mystic Krishnamurti often said, "Truth is a pathless land." Indeed, mystics have let go of the belief that there is only one right path, one right answer.

Continuing on this theme, we notice that sometimes the experiences and visions of mystics do not fully align with official Church teachings. Mystics admit this without embarrassment, confusion, or retraction. They trust the inner authority of their experience and do not insist others assent to it. Here is an example from Juliana of Norwich, a fourteenth-century English mystic. She wrote, "Holy Church taught me that sinners are sometimes deserving of blame and wrath, but in my visions, I could not see this in God....God is the goodness that cannot be wrathful....I saw no vengeance in God not for short time nor for long. God shows us no more blame than he does to the angels in heaven....I saw no wrath except in humans, and God forgives that in us."[4] Juliana simply reports her own experience without disparaging magisterial teaching. She does not contest theological teachings. She places her vision *beside* the teaching and leaves it at that. This is what Teilhard and other mystics do as we have seen throughout this book.

In his essay "The Phenomenon of Spirituality," Teilhard presents three components of a mystical spirituality:

1. It cannot help but emerge in us and in all that is.
2. It is irreversible and continually moving ahead, as well as "propagating itself interminably."
3. It is free of boundaries or limits and present in every moment and in all that happens.

We are seeing that mysticism is a knowing beyond what the brain can reach by thinking. What does a mystical moment look like in the brain? From a physical perspective, mystical experience activates the brain's center of attention and focus. At the same time, there is a numbing of our sense of orientation in space and time. During a mystical experience, there is considerably less activity in the primitive amygdala, and more activity in the hippocampus, part of the limbic system, that processes feelings and memories. Likewise, all this is engaged whenever we deeply focus or concentrate intensely. Similarly, there is a diminished sense of separation between the self and the world. This gives rise to the feeling of oneness, transcendence, and spaciousness. In addition, a mystical state quiets the speech and language centers of the brain, explaining its quality of ineffability. A mystical state also has bodily resonance, for instance, feeling, sensation, physical reactions, movement. It activates our entire being. Thus, it is more like a cosmic dance than a fixed stance.

Here are four specific qualities of mystical experience that were noted by psychologist of religion William James:

- A mystical experience is ineffable. It can't be described since it has more to do with *feeling into a mystery* than intellectual explanation.

Appendix

- Mystical consciousness goes beyond the discursive intellect. Mystical knowing is illumination, depth awareness.
- Mystical states are not enduring; they come and go.
- Mystical states may follow or grow from meditation or deep attention. Yet, a mystic always feels herself held by a higher power, receiving revelations from beyond ego/mind—what we can call grace.[5]

Mystical consciousness thus presupposes a dissolution of the ego mindset. A mystic's sense of personal identity has folded into universal consciousness, cosmic consciousness. She still exists as "this person" but knows her real identity is in a realm beyond personhood: "Rejoice that your names are written in heaven" (Luke 10:20).

A mystic sees, feels, finds, and is the More, the larger life beyond time and space. This allows more capacity for love, wisdom, and healing, that is, more capacity for God. A mystical sense of oneness extends to all our fellow humans. When I, as one with all, come to a nondual awareness, I suddenly realize that all the other beings in the world have the same capacity. This deepens my sense of union with everyone. True mystics therefore become more lovingly aware of others. As Thomas Merton showed us, mystics grow in concern for social justice. Indeed, there is no union with God without communion with humanity. There is no individual gain in the spiritual life without an ever-expanding loving kindness.

Mystics may experience pain and darkness, but at some time, they come to a sense of safety and repose. This may, of course, cycle to the dark night again. Mystics are no longer afraid of what might happen to them in life predicaments or from others since they trust that God is present in whatever happens, sometimes as comforter, sometimes as challenger.

Jesus, the supreme mystic, addresses God as "Our Father in heaven" (Matt 6:9) and yet likewise said, "The Father and I

are one" (John 10:30). He integrates the sense of divine as imma-
nent and transcendent. Some mystics continue to favor a strong
sense of God's transcendence, for instance as "the Beloved." On
the other hand, in *The Ascent of Mount Carmel*, St. John of the
Cross spoke this way: "God communicates to the soul his supernatural being so that the soul appears to be God himself and has
all that God himself has....All the things of God and the soul are
one in participant transformation, and the soul seems to be God
rather than the soul, and indeed *is* God by participation."[6] Using
a scientific model, we might say that within a molecule, a particle
is not a wave but it is not other than a wave. Likewise, we are not
God but we are also not other than God. In the mystics' view, God
and we are not identical but we are not separate.

> *Let creation repeat to itself again today, and tomorrow and*
> *until the end of time…*
> *"This is my Body."*

> —Pierre Teilhard de Chardin,
> *Writings in Time of War*

NOTES

Introduction

1. Richard Rohr, *What the Mystics Know: Seven Pathways to Your Deeper Self* (New York: Crossroad, 2015).

2. Teilhard de Chardin, *The Future of Man* (New York: Image, 2004), 186.

1. God in World and Matter

1. Arthur Green, *Radical Judaism: Rethinking God and Tradition* (New Haven, CT: Yale University Press, 2010), 20.

2. See David Richo, *When Catholic Means Cosmic: Opening to a Big-Hearted Faith* (Mahwah, NJ: Paulist Press, 2015).

3. In this and in other prayers in this book, I use the word "You" to refer to God. This is not meant dualistically. The "You" is the mystical you-in-me-and-in-all-things, the divine center of all that is and of all of us where there is only One of us.

2. A Spirituality of Evolution

1. William Shakespeare, *Richard II*, Act II, Scene 1, 270.

3. Love and Loving

1. Carl Jung, *Two Essays on Analytic Psychology*, Collected Works of C.G. Jung, vol.7, 2nd ed. (New Jersey: Princeton University Press, 1972).

2. James Finley, *The Awakening Call* (Notre Dame, IN: Ave Maria Press, 1984).

3. Teilhard de Chardin, *On Love and Happiness* (New York: Harper and Row, 1967), 3, 6.

4. Sri Aurobindo, *Thoughts and Glimpses* (Pondicherry: Sri Aurobindo Ashram Publications Department, 1973).

5. Anonymous fourteenth-century English Mystic, *The Cloud of Unknowing*, ed. and trans. William Johnston (New York, Random House, Image, 2012), 42.

6. See *Catechism of the Catholic Church*, § 460; St. Athanasius, *De inc.* 54, 3: PG 25, 192B; cf. also St. Irenaeus, *Adv. haeres*. 3, 19, 1: PG 7/1, 939.

7. Thomas Merton, *New Seeds of Contemplation* (New York: New Directions, 2007), 41.

8. See Richard Rohr, "Exploring and Experiencing *The Naked Now*" (Albuquerque, NM: CAC, 2012), MP3.

4. Our Inner Depths

1. Book of Thomas the Contender 138.7–19, in *Nag Hammadi Library*, 189.

2. St. Catherine of Genoa, *The Life and Doctrine of Saint Catherine of Genoa* (Grand Rapids, MI: Christian Classics Ethereal Library, 2000), 24.

3. *Nag Hammadi Library*, 490–500.

5. The Cosmic Christ

1. Gerard Manley Hopkins, "That Nature is a Heraclitean Fire and of the Comfort of the Resurrection," *Gerard Manley Hopkins: Poems and Prose* (London: Penguin Classics, 1985).

2. St. Irenaeus, *Against Heresies* 2.22.4.

Notes

6. The Sacred Heart of the Universe

1. Alice MacDonald, "For God So Loved the World: The Spirituality of Pierre Teilhard de Chardin" (Unpublished MA thesis, Loyola Marymount University, 1998).

2. See St. Augustine, *Confessions*, trans. John K. Ryan (New York: Image, 1960), bk. 3, ch. 2, 37.

3. Henry Miller, *The Colossus of Maroussi* (New York: New Directions, 1941), 70.

4. Fred Rogers ("Mister Rogers"), Acceptance speech when *Mr. Rogers' Neighborhood* won the 2001 Special Christopher Award.

5. William of Saint-Thierry, from the treatise *On Contemplating God*, Office of Readings, Advent: Week III, Monday, The Divine Office I: Advent, Christmastide & Weeks 1–9 of the Year, 102–3.

6. When Teilhard died in 1955, there was a picture on his desk of the Radiant Heart of Christ, personally inscribed with the words "My Litany."

7. The Divine Feminine and Mary

1. This distinction does not refer to traits or limitations in women or men but to energies in both women and men.

2. Apuleius, *The Golden Ass*, trans. Robert Graves (New York: Farrar, Straus and Giroux, 2009), 233.

3. Thomas Merton, "Dawn. The Hour of Lauds," in *In the Dark Before Dawn: New Selected Poems*, ed. Lynn R. Szabo (New York: New Directions, 2005), 65.

4. See David Richo, *When Mary Becomes Cosmic: A Jungian and Mystical Path to the Divine Feminine* (Mahwah, NJ: Paulist Press, 2016).

8. The Church and Religion

1. Pope Francis, "Letter to a Non-Believer," accessed November 4, 2016; http://w2.vatican.va/content/francesco/en/letters/2013/documents/papa-francesco_20130911_eugenio-scalfari.html.

2. Elaine Pagels, *The Gnostic Gospels* (New York: Vintage, 1989), 146.

9. The Eucharist

1. St. Augustine, "Augustine on the nature of the Sacrament of the Eucharist," *Sermon 272*.

2. *Catechism of the Catholic Church*, §795. See also St. Augustine, In Jo. ev. 21, 8: PL 35, 1568.

3. William T. Cavanaugh, *Torture and Eucharist: Theology, Politics, and the Body of Christ* (Hoboken, NJ: Wiley-Blackwell, 1998), 14.

10. The Power of Adoration

1. Teilhard de Chardin, *The Phenomenon of Man*, trans. Bernard Wall (New York: Harper and Row, 1959), 250.

2. George H. Tavard, *Poetry and Contemplation in St. John of the Cross* (Athens, OH: Ohio University Press, 1988).

3. St. John of the Cross, *The Spiritual Canticle and Poems* (London: Burns & Oates, 1978), 26.

4. Quoted in Henri de Lubac, *The Religion of Teilhard de Chardin* (New York: Image Books, 1968).

12. Shining Future, Glowing Expectancy

1. Origen, *De Principiis*, bk. 3, ch. 6, no. 5.

13. Infinite Treasures of Grace

1. See Hans Urs von Balthasar, "St. Therese's Little Way," accessed on November 7, 2016, https://www.crossroadsinitiative.com/media/articles/stthereselittleway/.

2. Pope Francis, "Homily: 2nd Vatican Council, Work of Holy Spirit but Some Want to Turn Back the Clock," April 15, 2013; http://en.radiovaticana.va/storico/2013/04/16/pope_2nd_vatican _council%2C_work_of_holy_spirit_but_some_want_to_tur/en1 -683419.

3. Jane Goodall, *Reason for Hope: A Spiritual Journey* (New York: Grand Central Publishing, 2000), 93.

Conclusion

1. Ursula King, "Rediscovering Fire: Religion, Science, and Mysticism in Teilhard de Chardin," accessed on November 8, 2016, http://www.earthlight.org/essay39_king.html.

Appendix

1. St. Cyril of Jerusalem, "Catechetical Homilies," in *Nicene and Post Nicene Fathers*, ed. Philip Schaff and Henry Wallace (New York: Cosimo, 2007), 7:33.

2. Augustine of Hippo, *Sermon 52*, 16.

3. Moses Maimonides, *The Guide for the Perplexed* (New York: Cosimo Books, 2007), I. 58.

4. See Julian of Norwich, *Showings*, ed. Edmund Colledge and James Walsh (Mahwah, NJ: Paulist Press, 1978), 266.

5. William James, *The Varieties of Religious Experience: A Study in Human Nature* (New York: Modern Library, 1929).

6. St. John of the Cross, *The Ascent of Mount Carmel*, bk. II, ch. 5, no. 7 (New York: Magisterium Press, 2015), 91.

OTHER PAULIST PRESS TITLES
BY THE AUTHOR

How to Be an Adult: A Handbook on Psychological and Spiritual Integration (1991) explores how we can evolve from the neurotic ego through a healthy ego to the spiritual self so that we can deal with fear, anger, and guilt. It offers ways that we can be assertive, have boundaries, and build intimacy.

How to Be an Adult in Faith and Spirituality (2011) explores and compares religion and spirituality with an emphasis on how they can both become rich resources for personal growth. We increase our understanding of God, faith, and life's plaguing questions in the light of mysticism, depth psychology, and our new appreciation of evolutionary cosmology.

How to Be an Adult in Faith and Spirituality (2012, compact disc). This set of four CDs is compiled from a workshop given at Spirit Rock Retreat Center in California on how to design and practice an adult spirituality. Each one examines the spiritual riches in religion and how to discern what is not in keeping with our adult evolution.

The Sacred Heart of the World: Restoring Mystical Devotion to Our Spiritual Life (2007) looks at the symbolism of the heart in world religious traditions and then traces the historical thread of Christian devotion to the Sacred Heart of Jesus into modern times. The book focuses on the philosophy and theology of Teilhard de Chardin and Karl Rahner to design a new sense of what devotion can be.

When Catholic Means Cosmic: Opening to a Big-Hearted Faith (2015) explores the impact of a cosmic dimension of our faith: when our faith becomes a trust without limit, our hope overflows with expectancy and our love stretches beyond all barriers. The book notes how our spirituality expands as we update our beliefs in accord with the best advances in psychology and science.

When Love Meets Fear: Becoming Defense-less and Resource-full (1997). Our lively energy is inhibited by fear, and we are so often needlessly on the defensive. This book considers the origins and healings of our fears of closeness, commitment, aloneness, assertiveness, and panic attacks so that we can free ourselves from the grip of fear that stops or drives us.

When Mary Becomes Cosmic: A Jungian and Mystical Path to the Divine Feminine (2016) takes a closer look at our cosmic vision of Mary. The Jungian archetype of the divine feminine as personified by Mary is built into the design of every human psyche. Her ancient titles reflect the marvelous qualities of our essential self. In fact, every religious truth and image is a metaphor for the potential in us and in the universe.

OTHER TITLES BY THE AUTHOR

Being True to Life: Poetic Paths to Personal Growth (Shambhala, 2009)

Coming Home to Who You Are: Discovering Your Natural Capacity for Love, Integrity, and Compassion (Shambhala, 2012)

Daring to Trust: Opening Ourselves to Real Love and Intimacy (Shambhala, 2010)

The Five Longings: What We've Always Wanted and Already Have (Shambhala, 2017)

The Five Things We Cannot Change and the Happiness We Find by Embracing Them (Shambhala, 2005)

How to Be an Adult in Love: Letting Love in Safely and Showing It Recklessly (Shambhala, 2013)

How to Be an Adult in Relationships: The Five Keys to Mindful Loving (Shambhala, 2002)

The Power of Coincidence: How Life Shows Us What We Need to Know (Shambhala, 2007)

The Power of Grace: Recognizing Unexpected Gifts on the Path (Shambhala, 2014)

Shadow Dance: Liberating the Power and Creativity of Your Dark Side (Shambhala, 1999)

When the Past Is Present: Healing the Emotional Wounds That Sabotage Our Relationships (Shambhala, 2008)

Wisdom's Way: Quotations for Meditation (Human Development Books, 2008)

You Are Not What You Think: The Egoless Path to Self-Esteem and Generous Love (Shambhala, 2015)